Poverty to Possibility:

Snapshots from a

Yorkshire Boyhood

Advance Praise for *Poverty to Possibility*

"When someone sets their heart, mind and soul on fulfilling a desired, very personal project, you can bet they will put every bit of their heart, every part of their mind and every ounce of their soul into that project. Diane Bailey-Boulet has done that in forensically researching and painstakingly unearthing the story of her father's childhood, capturing in great detail the near hopeless despair of the brutal poverty of 1930s industrial small-town Northern England and the struggles of a gifted, talented boy as he strove to unleash his potential in the face of crushing setbacks. The examples of encouragement and support in so many difficult moments and from so many different sources, provide an uplifting insight into human kindness. There are good people out there even in the darkest moments. There is a poignancy in its ending that is touching. Both in the moment of 'release' from that childhood and its environs and then in the achievements in adulthood on the other side of the world. A significant social history of a particular time, and also encouragement and inspiration to all, however difficult the start. It represents a wonderful tribute not only to her dad but to all those who suffered and fought for a better life. Not too many managed it!"

— Les Payne, former *Rotherham Advertiser* sports editor and *Sheffield Star* sportswriter and columnist (retired)

"I feel the love, warmth, and pride Diane has for her father in every word and turn of phrase. A wonderful tribute to a remarkable man."

— Fred Johnson, author of *Five Wars: A Soldier's Journey to Peace*

More Praise for *Poverty to Possibility*

"A compelling story of survival. This inspiring account of Harry Bailey's growing up made me think about how many children and their families around the world endure hardship and environmentally hazardous conditions, their dreams unfulfilled and their innate talents untapped. It also made me think about my own father and his largely unrecorded struggles."

— Joe Treasure, author of *The Book of Air; the male gaze; Besotted*

"A dynamic voice for the underdog. Harry Bailey's story reminds me that we each have the power to notice the potential in others and call it out, helping shape their lives--and ours--for the better."

— Ms. Sheri Riley, Author, *Exponential Living: Stop Spending 100% of Your Time on 10% of Who You Are*

"Like Harry Bailey in this story, reading as a child offered me relief and access to a wider world of possibilities where I could thrive. This is a powerful story about what happens when we empower ourselves and others to be the authors of our lives. Stepping into our stories helps us understand them and move from purpose to impact."

— Nick Craig, Author, *Leading from Purpose: Clarity* and *Impact to Act When It Matters Most*

Poverty to Possibility:

Snapshots from a

Yorkshire Boyhood

by Diane Bailey-Boulet

Printed in the United States of America

First Printing, 2020

ISBN: 978-1-7349242-4-4 (paperback)
ISBN: 978-1-7349242-5-1 (Kindle edition)
Library of Congress Control Number: 2020921741

Evensong Press
with assistance from A Page Beyond
Fishers, Indiana
www.APageBeyond.com

a page beyond

Ordering Information:

Special discounts are available on quantity purchases by corporations, associations, and others who purchase directly from the author. Contact Diane@ScaleExcellence.com for details.

Dedicated with love to Harry Bailey and his friend and mentor Horace Bailey—and to everyone who embraced their promise and helped them thrive.

Introduction

Diane Bailey-Boulet, June 2020

This book is in part my way of capturing some of the stories and images of my dad's childhood. I imagine each chapter as a snapshot or short film of sorts.

Harry Bailey beat the odds. He was born in early 1930 into a poor, working-class Yorkshire coal mining family in Britain's industrial north just as the tidal wave of economic calamity known as the Great Depression swept across the Atlantic from the United States to Britain and beyond, a tragedy that ultimately plunged millions worldwide into joblessness and despair.

He and his family lived at the bottom rung of the still-rigid social hierarchy of the British class system with its extremely limited choices and endemic, stunting poverty that held generations of his family and other working-class families firmly in its grip. It was a time where the poorest members of society were still expected to "know your place," do what you were told, and not to aspire to improving your life.

He lived a life far beyond all expectations for a child born into his situation and time, continuing his childhood education until he was 18. Most of his friends left school at 14 or 15 to work down a coal mine, like their fathers, brothers, uncles, grandfathers, and neighbors. Against staggering odds, he went to university and became a medical doctor. His career led him from Yorkshire to the United States, where he excelled as a radiologist, practiced medicine, and taught a generation of Harvard Medical School students in Boston, Massachusetts. He re-invented himself at 52, joining the United States Navy as a captain in the medical corps in San Diego, California.

To put these achievements in perspective, when he entered grammar school at 14 and finished at 18, *fewer than 4% of working-class British children were studying to that level.* The percentage of those who completed grammar school and then went on to university was even more minute. In short, he was an outlier. There were countless more children born into similar circumstances who did not have the opportunities or circumstances to express their greatest gifts and talents.

We have few photographs in the family of my dad from his childhood to early adulthood. The first is a small, worn, grainy, blurred amateur photograph of a small boy squinting as he looks at the camera, probably taken about 1933. My grandmother proudly displayed a photo in the family's front room of my dad as a little boy of six or so dressed in a white satin suit. I have never seen it—and don't know what became of it. Relatives remember it. We also have one lightly tinted 1941 school portrait photo--and a few more from the post-war years of his childhood.

My dad was born and raised at 21 Moxon's Yard, in Rawmarsh. His house was one of 12 in a side slip row of soot-encrusted brick "two-up, two-down" connected terraced houses where families shared walls with their neighbors on either side. Downstairs, each house had a sitting room to the front and small kitchen to the back, then two bedrooms upstairs accessed up a narrow staircase from the kitchen. The one cold water tap in the kitchen was the only running water in the house. There was a dark, narrow coal cellar below. The toilet, shared with neighbors, was outside in the back in a gravel yard. A laundry line was strung across the length of the back yard for Monday wash days. Coal was piled high, ready to be shoveled into the cellars to be use for heating the house. Sub-standard even when built in the Victorian era, various members of my family lived there for close to seven decades.

Moxon's Yard was leveled by the wrecker's ball in 1968, then paved over with concrete that was meant to be an improvement on what had stood there before. Today, in its newest incarnation built in the first part of this decade, a Tesco Express market, boxing gym, small shops, and a parking lot sit on the site. The space has taken on an entirely different use.

I have some early 20th century group photos of Moxon's Yard's inhabitants and plain exteriors—and a few color photos of its rooftops taken from Rawmarsh Hill from the mid-1960s. The rest of what I describe in this book is based on the recollections of family and friends.

Rawmarsh in the 1930s and 40s could also be like many children's lives today in places around the world where people live and work in communities where environmental degradation and dangerous, dead-end jobs endanger their families' health and well-being. Coal mining and heavily industrial communities continue to be demoralizing, unhealthy places to live and work.

Yet within each there are children with enormous potential if given a chance to thrive and succeed. If someone makes sure they know that they matter. *Because they do.*

The stories I've included come from or are inspired by what my dad told me growing up or from what family and friends told me about him, his character, his journey, and his challenges and triumphs from 1930 to 1948.

I seek to honor pivotal people in this story for their enormously positive influence in his life, people who saw something in a boy whose surroundings and circumstances were, at least on the surface, so wholly unpromising. They acted with empathy and compassion through words and actions, befriending, mentoring, and believing in him. I changed the names of people I wrote about who acted with cruelty. Their names matter less than the all-too-real archetype they represent. Harsh words, indifference, and cruelty leave scars that never fully heal.

My dad and his cousins Irene and Dorothy Dyson were musically gifted. Music played a key part in family life and how they found joy and each broke free from the limiting aspects of their circumstances. My dad was a chorister and bell ringer. He made a brave effort on the piano. Their stern, bullying maternal grandfather, John Edward Dyson, an intimidating figure, prodded them to learn to play the piano and have a "set piece" to perform. John Edward understood this: Musical skill and appreciation were an escape from the harsh daily realities, frustrations, and humiliations of life. My dad's set piece was Sir Edward Elgar's *Salut d'Amour*—or *Love's Greetings*.

This book is my tribute to a most-loving father and all the people who loved him, recognized his gifts, nurtured him, mentored him, stood by him, and let him know that he mattered.

Harry Bailey, the boy from Moxon's Yard, grew to be a true Renaissance man—musical, a gifted writer and artist, scientific, compassionate, an expert horticulturalist and orchid lover, and world traveler. He was and remains among the kindest, most generous and loving people I have ever known. As one of my close friends observed of my dad when I was a teen, "He lives and acts with all the virtues."

My dad's story energizes me and inspires me to be an ally and advocate for maximizing all human potential. His life story fuels my conviction that *every child deserves a chance to fulfill her or his potential on this earth.* I am a mentor and coach at heart, ever grateful to the people who saw, imagined, and supported a better future for and with Harry. Their love changed the trajectory of my family's history. Harry remains my north star and inspiration.

A Note on Dialect

Aspects of the Yorkshire and West Riding dialects are sprinkled lightly into these pages. I will not do the dialect justice and don't want to distract from the story.

I did not hear my dad's and grandparents' voices as "accented" growing up in Massachusetts. because they were what I knew first in my life and what I heard every day. They simply sounded like "Dad," "Grandma," and "Grandpa." To this day, hearing Yorkshire accents anywhere I am in the world is a huge comfort to me.

In reality, there is no "one" Yorkshire dialect. The dialect of the West Riding is probably the best-known, because of radio and television stories centered on the industrial communities there. It also differs from much of the rest of Yorkshire because it was influenced by the migration to the industrial communities by people from the Midlands. My great grandfather Bailey, for example, migrated from Shropshire to Yorkshire.

The dialects further north and west in Yorkshire, far less impacted by the Industrial Revolution migrations, have a distinct Scandinavian influence.

For a richer experience of the Yorkshire—including West Riding dialect, listen to:

"On Ilkla Moor Baht 'at"—or "On Ilkley Moor Without a Hat"—a popular folk song, is sung in the Yorkshire dialect and accent. It is the "unofficial" anthem of Yorkshire. We sang it enthusiastically as a family at home in Massachusetts as I grew up.

The audio recording and written examples available through the Yorkshire Dialect Society, founded in 1897. It is the world's oldest dialect society:

www.yorkshiredialectsociety.org.uk.

You can also follow Yorkshire Dialect Society on Facebook and Twitter.

Table of Contents

Hallelujah, Christmas in Rotherham

Rotherham, West Riding, Yorkshire, England

December 1929

It was Christmas Eve in Rotherham—a damp, biting cold winter's night not unlike the ones that led up to it, except that the rate of toxins spewing from hundreds upon hundreds of industrial smokestacks slowed and the ever-present coal-fire smog was slightly less intense. No amount of sulfurous coal dust could detract from the fact that Christmas, too, was in the air. Production at the many nearby steelworks and coal mining collieries ceased for a few days as workers, managers, and owners alike celebrated the coming of the birth of Jesus. On Doncaster Road, muffled passersby hastened off lit-up trams and headed home along the sidewalk, some with newspapers tucked under arm with the headline brightly hailing "*A Merry Christmas.*" Inside one small home along the way, the extended Dyson family filled the house's cramped front room to celebrate the excitement of the holiday. Such was the spirit of merriment that even anyone passing by the Foljambe Arms

15

Pub across the way could hear Christmas carols from the small house as voices and piano swelled together in harmony.

Inside the narrow soot-encrusted brick two-up, two-down row house, chestnuts roasted as the extra-bright coal fire glowed. Home-made red, green, and yellow paper chains hung across the room, sprigs of holly decorated the fireplace, and the pine sideboard dresser was loaded with plates of mince pies, coconut tarts, Wensleydale cheese, and sliced ham.

The birth of baby Jesus almost 1,930 years earlier was something to celebrate in this and millions more homes across Britain. On this Christmas Eve at the end of 1929, the anticipation of another birth in the family made the Biblical story of the holy child born in a manger all the more poignant: William Henry Bailey, a tall, soft-spoken, 29-year-old who hewed tons of coal a week for a living, and 28-year-old Edna (nee Dyson), his slightly-built, handsome, if not pretty, wife, had been married just over four year since August 1925. Their soon-to-be-first-born baby had been a long time coming. "Edna," gossips had whispered knowingly for too long, "wasn't able to have children." Now, in fact, the couple was looking forward to the birth of their own baby in February at the dawn of a new decade. The baby quick in Edna's belly was a source of pride and hopeful anticipation for the two—and on this night, this holy night, all their worries and cares receded as bright spirits mirrored one another in the gathered and growing family.

Now, as in all the Christmases the Dyson siblings could recall, John Edward Dyson, Edna's father, hosted—some would say he *held court*—as his growing extended family of offspring, their spouses, and grandchildren turned to each other and away from the cares of the world. At least for a few days all would be aglow as everyone celebrated Christmas between their various homes. With the fire's warmth, music in the air, and the room filled with merriment it was a scene reminiscent of a Victorian post card.

John Edward Dyson—small in stature yet menacing in presence—lived and breathed music. Anyone born into or marrying into his family was expected to embrace making music, whether it came naturally or not. Each year the annual Christmas Eve get-together reached its climax when John Edward, a coal miner by caste and musician and brass band conductor by talent, sat at his piano, as he did every year, to conduct and accompany the family in George Frederic Handel's glorious and joyful "Hallelujah" chorus from the *Messiah*.

Hallelujah! Hallelujah! Hallelujah! Hallelujah!
Hallelujah!
For the Lord God Omnipotent reigneth.
Hallelujah! Hallelujah! Hallelujah! Hallelujah!
King of kings, and Lord of lords,
King of kings, and Lord of lords,
And Lord of lords,
And He shall reign,
And He shall reign forever and ever,
King of kings, forever and ever,
And Lord of lords...
Hallelujah! Hallelujah!
And He shall reign forever and ever,
King of kings! and Lord of lords!
And He shall reign forever and ever,
King of kings! and Lord of lords!
Hallelujah! Hallelujah! Hallelujah! Hallelujah!
Hallelujah!

John Edward led his offspring with authority, singing robustly in a rich baritone over his sons Harold and Johnny and Rowland and sons-in-law William and Joe. Edna and her sisters Elsie and Nellie, younger half-sister Lucy, and sister-in-law Kath carried the soprano and alto parts. The sounds swelled as the stanzas switched from motet, to chorale, to fugue forms through the lyric's staunch acclamations from the ancient book of *Revelations*. Among the women, Edna's rich, bright soprano voice was the strongest and sunniest of them all as the music called upon them to raise their voices to rise ever higher through the repetitions of "King of Kings and Lord of Lords." Everyone pulled out their finest harmonies and vocal stops to form the rousing final crescendo at the final *"Hallelujah!"* It was their finest moment year after year.

The toddlers in the room, cousins Irene and "young" Elsie, sat in their fathers' arms basking in the occasion, fascinated by the rich voices of their parents, aunts, and uncles swelling in harmony and Granddad Dyson basking in the glory of the sound he had conjured from his offspring.

Even Emily, John Edward's common-law wife, who moved in as his housekeeper soon after he was newly widowed, seemed to have a small smile on her face, even as she endured the never-ending low-burning hostility of John Edward's bereaved children from his first wife, Lucy, on this and all family occasions.

After the singing, everyone settled in where they could in the small room to tuck into the pies. For all Emily's transgressions—real and imagined—in the eyes of John Edward's first four children, she always put on a beautiful spread of mince pies, coconut tarts, and punch that made the evening special.

Once he finished conducting, John Edward reverted to form, standing up from the piano, taking his silver-tipped black cane in hand, assuming his usual stance as the stern, autocratic, always potentially explosive patriarch of the Victorian style. Edna had never known any different, just that throughout her childhood her father had had a habit of letting drink get a hold of him after successful competition outings with his brass band, returning home the worse for wear and bringing everyone into his misery, and too often belittling his children and ignoring their pursuits or their own talents. If he had ever been gentler when her mother was living Edna couldn't remember it. Her father had long since sealed his heart off to her and her two sisters and brother, especially in their greatest moment of grief and despair. He was little if any better later with her half-sister Lucy and half-brothers Johnny and Rowland.

But now, with Christmas in the air and the loving support of William as they anticipated parenthood, Edna was content to enjoy Christmas. She looked forward to her own future as a mother and knew William would be a loving and very different kind of father than her own.

Throughout the evening, given her condition, swollen feet, and swollen belly, Edna, for the first time in her life, was granted a place on the settee across from her father in his special chair. She basked in the attention of her sisters as they took turns bringing her mince pies and guessing the sex of the baby based on Edna's size. "Maybe you're having twins!" exclaimed Nellie, "You're certainly carrying a big one—or two!" Edna laughed nervously, but quietly hoped to herself that there was just one baby inside her and that it would be a boy. If he were, he'd be John Edward's first grandson. Perhaps then, at last, her father would be a little kinder to her and see her worth. Just a few kinds words were all she longed for from him.

Whatever the case, in another year's time the baby would be part of the family gathering, and William would be the proudest father in the room. There was plenty to celebrate.

Rawmarsh

The largest rainfall on record in Britain—twenty-seven inches in four months—the equivalent of what typically fell over the first eight-and-a-half months of a year, drenched Britain between October 1929 and January 1930. Sometimes it fell as a warm drizzle, other times in torrential downpours, other times as icy sleet and snow. Ancient villages flooded, cattle drowned, rail lines and bridges washed away, and rivers and canals overflowed—unable to contain the abnormal volume of water. The damage was considerable, especially as homes flooded and people with very little watched that little become even less. Those living in the worst housing dealt with an added misery of leaking roofs and walls and open sewage overflowing from outdoor toilets.

In Yorkshire's West Riding, nestled in the valleys between the Rother, Dearne, and Don Rivers, the village of Rawmarsh was like most other coal mining pit towns, a mining

23

community consisting of a main High Street with off-shoot streets of row upon row of linked-together grimy, squat, soot-blackened terraced houses that had been built in haste of cheap, rough, inelegant brick on what since ancient times had been England's green and pleasant lands. Most of these houses were built in parallel rows on either side of the narrow cobbled or gravel streets, set back to back with houses on other streets. In all cases the houses and the families within them—most of whom migrated to these industrial heaps after being uprooted from increasingly mechanized agricultural communities from across England a generation or two before--shared foul-smelling privies and poor air circulation that easily led to the spread of disease.

The floor plan for the houses was the same in all: Two rooms downstairs—a cramped lounge to the front and a poky, poorly ventilated kitchen to the back. From the kitchen a narrow staircase led up to two bedrooms upstairs. The dwellings were miserly in size and appointments, sub-standard even when first thrown up in the 1870s and 1880s, the most glorious days of the British Empire, as the urban working-class population exploded, pouring into industrial cities, human cogs in a mighty economy.

William and Edna lived second from the bottom of one of their row of houses at number 21 Moxon's Yard. Like the rest of the yard's two-up and two-down houses, it offered damp, cold living conditions, especially when ice formed inside the windows in winter. Year 'round, sulphur dioxide-filled soft-coal-fired smoke from thousands upon thousands of home chimney plus soot particles and chemical fumes from thousands more industrial smokestacks belched filth from the nearby collieries, factories, steelworks, and railways. Plentiful soot fell and settled like black snowflakes around and upon them. Residents could fill a bucket with shovels full of the ash that settled in the roadside gutters, especially closer to the pig-iron blast furnaces down Rawmarsh Hill at Parkgate. Like everyone around them, Edna and William breathed it in, and, as a matter of course, spat and coughed it up as its particles settled deeply and dangerously into their lungs.

Large, menacing slag heaps of mines waste, shaped like disfigured pyramids, blighted the area and, with the potential to collapse and bury everything and everyone around them, endangered those who lived close by. This toxic mix in which so many were consigned to live and raise families as they struggled to survive, spewed into the air, the rivers, and canals, which for years now had been nothing less than open sewers devoid of life. The West Riding's pit towns and cities had the highest incidence of life-stunting and shortening bronchial ailments in the country. Scientists had determined Rawmarsh to be the among the most polluted communities in all of England, worse even than London with its infamous "pea souper" sometimes yellowish, greenish, or blackish fogs.

Now, with winter's short days, a depressing miserly ration of daylight filtered through pollution and the north-facing, small, drafty, 12-paned sash windows at the front of the house. The cold, damp air flowed through the rotting frames. The repeated exposure to these not-quite-freezing indoor conditions inflamed Edna's and William's small blood vessels, leading to the swelling, itchiness, red patches, and painful blistering in their extremities known as *chilblains*.

Britain's still rigid class hierarchy—where hereditary transmission pre-determined one's "rank," "station in life", education, and occupation meant that as members of semi-and unskilled manual laboring families, William, Edna, and nearly everyone they knew were second from the bottom rung of society. At the dawn of 1930, the inadequacy, age, and structurally degraded condition of 21 Moxon's Yard was no different than thousands upon thousands more houses like it across England's industrial north. The house had no electricity. There was gaslight downstairs. Candlelight sufficed for upstairs. There was one cold water tap in the kitchen. Its roof and some of its walls leaked, cracking and staining the plaster on the walls. The red linoleum-covered flooring sloped and creaked. William and Edna were like all their nearest neighbors, family, and friends: Poor families with no other choices but to continue to work day in, day out to pay rent each week to live in the decrepit dwellings while their landlords exacted high rents on crumbling houses that needed to be condemned.

As conditions in much of southern and midlands of England improved in the 1920s and new houses and housing estates grew after the Great War of 1914-1918, Rawmarsh and pit towns like it across the industrial north were largely unaltered, fossilized from a scarcity of new opportunity and new housing. Countless families struggled in a never-ending battle against industrial waste and squalor that continuously threatened to close in on them.

Given the conditions on Moxon's Yard, baby on the way or not, like every other miner's wife and despite her swelling belly, growing discomfort, and a constant undertow of anxiety, Edna worked through a relentless schedule of daily household chores. Like all the women she knew around her, she had from an early age internalized the lessons that came with her station in life: Cleanliness and godliness were the prerequisites of pride and respectability, the all-important currency of their survival in a society where everyone was born into and expected to know his or her place and stay there. Consequently, Edna set about her daily chores as a woman proud that her home was as clean and comfortable as possible for her husband and, shortly, for her baby too.

Edna's host of household chores followed a rigid weekly routine the same as all the women she knew. Each week included cooking, baking, and the constant chore of heating water, then more water for washing up and bathing. Her work continued with cleaning the soot-streaked windows inside and out, sweeping and dusting, scrubbing, making the bed, darning and mending William's underground pit clothes, cleaning the privy she and William shared with his mother and brother next door, and hauling coal up from the cellar to keep the fire going to take some of the sting out of the damp, cold conditions.

There were even harder chores to be done: Edna had to be the manager of the meager family income from William's weekly pay packet, the amount of which fluctuated with each week. Shopping for bargains was a must and deciding who would be paid, when, and how much was another mind-boggling task. There was only so much money. On a bad week Edna had to decide whether to pay the rent man, the insurance agent, the milkman, feed the gas meter, or pay the doctor. Most weeks she had to tell at least one of the money collectors who regularly came 'round that she would need to pay something the following week instead or pay them less than they came to collect. She balanced a fragile and difficult economic equation. The one relief from this constant worry was the arrival of the pile-high ton of concessionary coal that came two-to-three times a year from William's work in the pit. This was tipped onto the pavement in the yard to be shoveled down the cellar shoot by the family for storage. The homes fires, at least, would keep burning as long as work at the pit was steady.

Then there were the real back-breaking household chores. Monday was wash day every week, which started at the crack of dawn with drawing gallons of water from the one tap in the house into a large copper set pot and then heating the water. She used the water for washing and rinsing, mangling, and then hanging the family laundry to dry on the rope line that stretched between two community clothes posts in the back yard. Next she starched and ironed the dried shirts, dresses, and bedding. With all the winter rain, more often than not Edna hung the clothes inside from rope lines strung across the kitchen, fastening them on with pine wood pegs. She hung socks and smaller pieces on wooden racks next to the fire in the front room.

Edna's weekly ritual also included black leading and polishing the metal fireplace which was the first thing to catch the eye of any visitor—so, like every other home her fireplace had a permanent gleam, even if nothing else in the outside world surrounding the family did.

Upon William's return home from work and a loving kiss of relief each time, Edna made sure that there was sufficient hot water to pour into the large tin bath that hung on a hook outside the back door. As she poured water into a pitcher, William brought in the bath and placed it before the fire upon the handmade pegged hearth rug. As soon as he was in the bath Edna washed the dried sweaty coal dust from William's back, then rinsed the mixture of coal dust from his hair and back. Her final part in this working day ritual was to place a warm towel over his sore shoulders as he stood up to dry himself. By the time he had dried and dressed and had drained and re-hung the bath on the outside wall Edna had put away his pit clothes and put their dinner on the table. After William had said grace they would eat.

Edna, like all the women she knew, ritualistically kept the outside of her house as clean as she kept the interior. This meant first scrubbing, then scouring of the stone window sills and doorstep with the penny yellow scouring stone, then lining the doorstep edge white with donkey stone—made of limestone, cement, and bleach—a ritual that housewives all across the north carried out, partly because it made the step less slippery, partly because Edna could exchange gossip with her neighbors who were also doing the same chore at the same time, and, perhaps most importantly, to demonstrate to neighbors and anyone else the cleanliness of the home, no matter the filthy surroundings. These were the tasks that taxed Edna's strength as she found it more difficult to get up off her knees. Nevertheless, she repeated this exhausting ritual day after day and week after week, as did all the miners' wives in Moxon's Yard and beyond throughout the least privileged households in the shrouded pit communities in the valleys of the Don, Rother, and Dearne rivers.

Now, with Christmas well behind them and the short supply of daylight in winter days the constant, in between scrubbing, mending, polishing, cooking, shopping, and all the tasks she carried out, Edna, already nervous by nature, waited anxiously for the day her baby would arrive. She could hear the cries of baby Derek Cooper coming from next door and his mother Mary Ellen trying to soothe him. Soon Edna, too, would be soothing a wailing infant and would bounce a little baby upon her knee.

Gnawing worry, difficult to ignore, was not unique to Edna, 'though, given the earlier tragedy in her childhood, it may have been more pronounced in her. All mining families faced a grim reality as the menfolk headed to work each day. Pit work was back-breaking, dangerous, dead end, and, not infrequently, deadly. Each day William and all miners faced the dangers of *fire damp* explosions—caused by a deadly build-up of methane gas and hydrogen, asphyxiating *choke damp*, and *white damp* from hydrogen sulfide and carbon monoxide from exposure to the air causing coal in the mine to burn slowly. Added to these dangers, roof collapses, injury or death by run-away loaded tubs, poor ventilation, a lack of oxygen, cage crashes descending to the coal face, broken limbs, shattered skulls, and the specter of gasping for every breath, then dying from *pneumoconiosis*—black lung disease—from years of breathing coal dust to make a living.

Every Rawmarsh mining family knew someone who went to work at the pit in the morning and never made it home—or who went in one piece and came home broken in some physical or spiritual way. Premature death was a fact of life, something Edna and William had been all too familiar with as children, when a miner died every six hours in a British coal mine while another was seriously injured every two hours.

Every coal mining community had more than their share of paraplegics, men with missing limbs, black lung, and families where death had made young widows and fatherless children commonplace.

And yet miners, and by default their families, were all but universally ignored or worse yet, despised or scorned by the upper classes whose lives of ease and comfort were fuelled by coal, whose homes were kept warm, whose transport was quick, and whose industries prospered because of the works of the miners who worked hundreds of yards underground. Close to four years after the Great Strike of 1926, mining families had seen their economic circumstances worsen substantially. It began when Germany began to send "free" coal to France and Italy in 1925 as reparations from the Great War while Britain returned to the gold standard, making the pound sterling too strong on the world market. British exports fell and coal prices plummeted. Amid this reality, mine owners were determined to normalize their profits at the expense of the miners. Mine owners joined forces to cut wages from an average £6.00 to £3.90 per week. They did this while increasing miners' working hours and enacting district wage agreements. This led to the lock-out of 800,000 miners when they refused the pit owners' terms. In May 1926, the Trade Union Council called on all British workers to strike in solidarity with the miners. It was unsuccessful. Prime Minister Stanley Baldwin's Conservative government passed the Trades Dispute Act, labeling general strikes as revolutionary and illegal. The mine owners' draconian wage cuts and increased hours stuck.

William and Edna had married in August 1925, the beautiful yet unsettling summer before the failed Great Strike. A stop-gap mining wage subsidy only delayed a looming crisis. In 1926, mine owners expected to continue extracting their customary profits by slashing the wages of the miners. The General Strike of 1926 impacted the nation, but nowhere did it hit harder than in mining families. By fall 1926, miners' bargaining power, wages, and job security sank to levels lower than they had been before the strike. What few mine owners, union leaders, or miners, if any, could see was that the overall coal industry was structurally sick, unsound, subsiding drastically in parts like the ground above the coal seams. The fewer miners working longer hours for less pay led to an increase in productivity that benefitted the mine owners.

William was among the hundreds of thousands of miners who had no choice but to accept the drastic wage cut and longer hours and return to the coal seam. Employment levels in the mines never returned to what they had been before the strike, with many miners permanently displaced. He was one of Britain's one million miners who were looked down upon, in fact despised as uncouth and uncultured, as "the other" within their own country, even as they worked at great risk hundreds of feet beneath the earth's surface, at times waist-high in cold water, other times in intense heat, almost naked, crawling on hands and knees through narrow passages miles underground to reach coal seams. He and the many more like him mined the coal that fuelled great fortunes for some, warmed great cities, grand homes and small cottages across the land, fired the ships' turbines that sent Britain's exports across the globe and kept the exchequer and Royal Navy afloat, and fired industry, digging the fuel that made the intense heat for steelmaking possible, powered the looms of Lancashire's cotton and Yorkshire's woollen mills, and provided countless jobs and comforts to millions of other Britons. True to Ivor Novello's exhortation in the patriotic song from the Great War, they kept the home fires burning.

♦ ♦ ♦

Just under four miles from Moxon's Yard stood the elegant and imposing Wentworth Woodhouse—the largest private house in Britain. The stately house boasted a 600-foot façade, longer than that of Buckingham Palace, and longer than any house in Europe. The house covered close to four acres, standing in all its grandeur in a 15,000-acre park. A Georgian splendor, it had 365 rooms—a room for every day of the year—plus 1000 windows and five miles of corridors and underground passageways. It was said to have been Jane Austen's inspiration for Pemberley, the grand home of Fitzwilliam Darcy in *Pride & Prejudice*. Its massive art collection included paintings by Flemish master Anthony Van Dyck, portraitists Sir Joshua Reynolds, Daniel Mytens, John Hoppner, and Thomas Lawrence, along with collections of works by landscape painter Claude Lorrain. Perhaps most spectacular of all was the close-to-life-size, commanding equine portrait of the pure-bred Arabian horse *Whistlejacket* by animal portraitist George Stubbs.

The 7th Earl "Billy" Fitzwilliam and family lived there along with eighty-five indoor servants, entertaining royalty including King George V and Queen Mary in 1912 in its close to 125,000 square feet of living space. The royal visitors had required 76 bedrooms for their entourage. There was no shortage of space.

The 15,000-acre estate also employed 300 to tend to its outdoor spaces—including acres of formal gardens. The Fitzwilliam Estate sat on the Great Barnsley Seam, which produced the coal that fuelled the family's vast wealth. The estate included 120 collieries employing 115,000 men, plus mineral rights and a priceless art collection. Closely connected to the land and the people dependent on the estate, the Earl Fitzwilliam was a caring employer with a "soft touch" in contrast to the vast majority of mine owners, most of whom had no connection to the area. His mines were the safest in the area. During the 1926 strike he fed his striking miners and led them in polo matches with the pit ponies on the Wentworth Estates. He was, as a result, well-loved by his workers. His approach was in stark contrast to the ruthless owners of mining companies who were intent on extracting all the coal wealth they could, no matter what the high human cost in death, injury, and despair was to miners on poverty wages and their families.

◆ ◆ ◆

Now, at the dawn of the 1930s, as each work day passed, Edna stopped whatever she was doing as the bells sounded from the nearby St. Mary's Parish Church tolling two-o'clock, reminding her of the end of the morning shift at the local collieries and Parkgate Iron & Steel Works. William would make his way home soon. She coaxed her swollen body from her chair and put aside the mending. She put away the nearly completed baby booties and afghan she was knitting. She moved to the kitchen to prepare William's dinner. Her heart beat a little faster as she listened for the reassuring, slow, steady sound of heavy pit boots on the grit and dirt yard steps. Some knew that it would be at least one hour before she heard the doors of the Farmeries, Waistnedges, Parkins, Charlesworths, and Coopers open and close. This signaled that their men had returned home from the pit. At six-feet tall, William had a stride and gait distinct among the men on the yard. Her mind could only achieve some semblance of peace when she could hear his steps grow louder and louder as he drew near, then stopped at the door. This would assure her that her husband of nearly four years had returned safely from another death defying, back breaking day of toil in the bowels of the earth.

William made his way home on foot from one exacting shift after another, each of which left him totally exhausted. His clothes were covered in dried-on coal dust that blackened his fair skin and formed black rings around his soft green-blue eyes. It was the only work routine he knew and one he had done every shift since he left school at fourteen. Britain and Germany were at war when William first started in the mines by driving pit ponies underground to add to his family's purse and as a patriot for king and country. The country depended on coal to fight the war. Shortages threatened the war effort. William followed his father into mining, like every lad he knew from school had. Like his father and uncle before him, over the years he had hewn thousands of tons of coal, on his knees, with no more than a pick and shovel, the strength and power of his sinewy body and arms. It was all he knew. It was all most boys in the Rother Valley knew--all that was available for the likes of boys like him. In fact, when William went down the mine in 1915, 90% of coal mined was cut by hand. Depending on the mine and the region, miners were paid through different systems. If miners worked a "stint," it meant that they had to clear a certain amount of the coal face or their pay was docked. More often in the Rother Valley, William—

and the other miners—filled tubs, put brass tags in with their assigned numbers on them for the coal to be counted by someone, then they were paid accordingly.

Now, 15 years later, as he trudged home through the winter afternoon dusk in the damp and bitter cold that cut to the bone, he watched his warm breath turn to vapor in the cold air as his thoughts turned to his impending fatherhood. He was nervous about making ends meet with another mouth to feed, but he resolved to provide as best as he could for Edna and their child. He loved children and was already fond of his nephews and nieces.

Good or bad working conditions determined how much coal he could extract and take home in wages. Most days he crawled on hands and knees through water to and from the coal face, Good conditions didn't mean that things were any easier. Paying their way and making ends meet was a constant struggle. But bad conditions guaranteed that making ends meet was even more difficult and dangerous because the coal seams themselves were the more treacherous ones.

Now, as winter's icy grip took firm hold in the Rother Valley just a short time before his child was due, times were even more uncertain: Across the stormy Atlantic, the American economy had collapsed just months earlier with the September 1929 stock market crash on Wall Street. The massive shock wave was now on a collision course toward Britain and the economies of Europe. Everyone was apprehensive. Still, from the Rother Valley, the problems in far-away America seemed worlds away.

On most of these cold, wet January afternoons Edna's mother-in-law, Frances Bailey, dropped by from next door to check on Edna, saying, "Come next door and have a cup of tea by the fire, love. Put your worries aside and your feet up a bit." This was a welcome break for both women from their housework and its frequently isolating effects.

Frances knew only too well the fear and anxiety that concentrated the mind of a miner's wife until her man returned safely home, each day hoping for hope that she would never hear the urgent clang-clang-clang of fireplace pokers being struck against fireplace hobs from household to household as wives up and down streets, rows, and yards across the town spread the dreaded news of a pit disaster in a primitive but effective kind of Morse Code. Now widowed, Frances had gone through the very same anxiety many times, first with her own father and brothers, then her husband, and now her sons. Frances's own husband, also named William, had died prematurely at 58, not quite two years earlier, from a cerebellar haemorrhage—or bleeding into the brain. The coroner at the inquest and on the death certificate made a point to connect this to *chronic interstitial Nephritis* that started with an infection that spread from "a slight injury to his hand" sustained in his dangerous work at Aldwarke Colliery. He cut his hand there in October of 1927. The infection from it spread, worsened to Cellulitis, then led to an agonizing months-long illness and death seven months later in May of 1928. William senior—husband, father, grandfather, brother, son—became another tragic mining statistic from work that felled the strongest of men and boys through debilitating injuries and death. Fear and anxiety hung in the air around mining families day in and day out.

In her youth, Frances had been a fine, tall, fun, big-hearted Yorkshire lass, a "grand lass." Like all the girls she knew she left school at 14 to work as a domestic servant, putting her hands to scrubbing pots and pans, peeling pound after pound of potatoes, hauling coal to light home fireplaces, a job that cut short her education. But it was a cut above the abuses, danger, and soul-destroying monotony of factory work. A job in service was a badge of honor for a girl: It meant that she was seen as trustworthy and a credit to her family. As was common with her contemporaries, Frances was a one-man woman. No man would replace the husband she had met and loved so young. Together they raised four children, all of whom survived to adulthood—Maggie, Ethel, William, then Leonard.

Back when the Great War was in full and devastating force, Frances had put on a brave face when her tall, lanky, gentle-spirited son William left school on his 14th birthday in October 1915 to join his father down the pit at Aldwarke Colliery. There, father and son toiled in the depths of the Silkstone Seam to mine coal that made for excellent steel making and household heating. There was nothing else for young William but to follow in his dad's footsteps. He was too young to join the armed services and fight in the Great War, 'though he wanted to join a Yorkshire regiment or perhaps the Navy to be like the older lads and men he looked up to. When he left with his dad for the pit that first day, Frances hugged him, handed him his snap tin filled with bread and drippings, passed him his water bottle, then watched and waved as the two Williams walked up Moxon's Yard. When they were out of sight, she went inside to let her true feelings out: She wept, wanting her son to be safe, wanting something better for him than to leave school because there were no other choices. He clearly had great intelligence and a knack for learning. She felt the weight of a community and nation sending so many young men to war to not return. In his first weeks on the job, Frances never let on to her son that she heard him weeping in his sleep from exhaustion and the saddening realization that his brightness and intellectual abilities were of no value to those who employed him only for his muscle and dispensability.

Now, given her life's experiences and a kind heart, Frances was maternal and protective for the vulnerable, especially her daughter-in-law, despite of or because of Edna's frequent bouts of sorrowful pessimism. Both the Baileys and Dysons had lost men to the dangers of work at Aldwarke Main Colliery. Even though they were a generation apart in age, the two women shared in common that they had both left school at 14 to work as domestic servants, cooking and scrubbing and hauling in homes far more well-appointed than their own. Even as much of the world changed around them, it seemed that in so many ways their "station in life" had not and would not. At least they were both spared the dangers and tedium of factory work.

Edna was grateful to Frances for the invitations to rest with a cup of tea for a while, yet viewed her mother-in-law with a mixture of emotions: She was envious of Frances's lighter nature—and lived each day pulled down by the undertow of wishing that her own mother, Lucy, were close by. Edna witnessed her own mother suffer through, then die of tuberculosis at 33, a disease that spread all too easily in crowded slums and which killed young women at higher rates. Edna had just turned 7 a few weeks before her mother's death. Family members liked to recall with pride that before marrying John Edward Dyson, Lucy was "raised as a lady," did fine embroidery, had never worked, and "had connections"—spoken about in hushed tones—to an important family. Some would whisper that she had married well beneath her station. By the time Lucy had lived in the harsh, crowded conditions of mining families, carried and delivered four children, and dealt with the cares and worries of that life, most traces of Lucy's earlier life and greater comforts were gone. Many family members believed that the event that triggered Lucy's illness was the horrific death of Mark Dyson, her brother-in-law, in the 1904 Aldwarke Main pit disaster: Seven miners headed to work in a cage elevator died as the 3.5-inch circumference rope to the cage elevator they were descending in snapped, sending the metal cage and the men in it plummeting to the depths, where they crashed at the shaft bottom. The retrieved mangled bodies of the men entangled in the cage wreckage were all but unrecognizable from one another. For Lucy the shock of her brother-in-law's horrific death was made worse by the realization that John Edward, who always went to work with his brother, had, unusually, been late for work that morning, missing the fateful 5:20 a.m. descent and gruesome death.

Whether the pit crash triggered her illness or not, Lucy had suffered the all-too-common fate of poor young women of child-bearing years living in the slums of the Rother Valley. She was worn down by the structural societal barriers and hardships of a life of inadequate means, all-but-non-existent choices, substandard housing, and the indifference and scorn of too many of the better-off in society to the plight of the working poor. Giving birth to and raising her children in overcrowded, slum-like conditions had depleted her resources and made her vulnerable to disease. Tragedy had crushed Lucy's spirit.

For Edna, life was sorrowful enough as she watched her mother cough up blood and waste away. Lucy was admitted to Smedley's Hydro, an imposing hydropathy center founded in the mid-19th century and which welcomed many celebrated figures, among them Robert Louis Stevenson. An "unnamed benefactor" covered the costs of her care there for reasons that would only emerge in hushed whispers among adults in the family. It was set upon a broad slope in the cleaner, dryer air and green hills of Matlock, a spa town 30 miles from her husband and children at home. The splendid views of the Derbyshire Dales, within close walking distance of the beautiful river, rock, and wooded landscapes of Matlock Dale, Matlock Bath, and Cromford, were of little consolation. The treatments at Matlock postponed, but ultimately failed to save her from death.

At her funeral, pretty painted flowers decorated the pamphlets printed for the service and a solid headstone with a delicate floral motif marked her grave on the slope of

Rawmarsh Cemetery, just outside of the enclosed St. Mary's Parish Church. The understated elegance of her grave was one consolation her children could be proud of as they lay real blossoms there.

Edna's life and the lives of her two older sisters, Elsie and Nellie and brother Harold were never the same. Their father John Edward, trapped as a miner by caste, was a talent a highly accomplished, self-taught musician who could play any instrument he turned his eye to. He composed music and conducted his brass band with aplomb. He was a sought-after competition judge, too. But as a father, with Lucy gone, he was a terrifying man, unable to see beyond his own self-pity, frustration, broken hope, and heartbreak to help his shattered children. After Lucy's death, consumed with pain and indifferent to his children's, he in turn struck fear into his children's hearts with his rages, showed no empathy for their despair and needs. He belittled or ignored their talents and aspirations as he tried in vain to deny his own anguish, confusion, and humiliation at his own limited choices. He had been unable to provide a better life for his wife, who he truly loved, in the most powerful country at the heart of the greatest empire on earth.

Adding further to the Dyson children's pain and emotional neglect, Lucy's mother Emma, their maternal grandmother, made a point of dressing in her most-regal attire to pay a visit to her four grandchildren at their home after her daughter's death to declare that she was disowning them. She told them in no uncertain terms that she would have nothing more to do with them and no longer considered them family. She disapproved of their father. She held true to the cutting vindictiveness of her words for the rest of her comfortable life.

John Edward's most glorious achievement came after Lucy's death: He threw his energies further into music and conducted a prize-winning brass band and judged band competitions. He conducted the Rotherham Main Colliery band, which won the Grand Shield at the 1910 Crystal Palace competition in London. It became a source of family pride that his photograph, for many years to come, was displayed in one of London's greatest expedition and music venues.

Frances had strong emotional resources and a lighter nature. She was from a stalwart, generations-old Rawmarsh family, the Wilsons. She was born and grew up in a caring family in a modest but harmonious home in a terraced house on the steep slope of Church Street with its still mostly bucolic views of Greasbro' Tops, a short distance from Moxon's Yard. She met the young man who became her husband on Church Street, when he had found lodging next door to her family. She first set eyes on him just hours after he had walked for days with his brother Zach, both in their late teens, some 90 miles over eight days from Dawley, Shropshire in the late 1890s to seek work in the coal mines.

Life had brought together two very different women into one family. Yet they, like their families, shared the common experience of lives of few or limited choices at the bottom rungs of British society. They shared a wall between their homes, made what they could of what they had, and both looked forward to the arrival of the baby. Edna was eager to be a mother, and Frances was ready to love and care for a new grandchild after the anguish of losing and mourning her beloved husband.

◆ ◆ ◆

Nature set into relentless motion as January turned the corner to February. On a Friday morning as she absentmindedly pressed her index finger into toast crumbs on a breakfast plate at the kitchen table, Edna felt the first urgent wave of sharp cramping of early labor. William had left for the pit a few hours before. She dropped everything to make her way next door to her mother-in-law's. When Frances saw her wide, terrified eyes and pale face she didn't need words from Edna to know anything more. She gathered her shawl and pulled an apple that she was roasting in the fire out of the flames, stabbing it with a long fork and placing it on a plate on the hearth. She helped Edna back home, easing into a chair by the fire, and covered her in a blanket. She heated more water to make tea. What started as mild cramping intensified through the afternoon into waves of sharp pain, the kind that every new mother had heard about and which lived up to its reputation as being excruciating and unlike any pain felt before.

Edna's waves of labor pain grew in intensity and frequency over the next hours into the evening. Frances had gone next door to tell Mary Ellen Cooper about Edna's condition, and Mary Ellen scooped up baby Derek and headed toward Dr. O'Connell's Rawmarsh Hill surgery to seek their help in contacting the midwife. Frances stationed herself at Edna's feet, gently rubbing them and talking in soothing tones to her daughter-in-law. Edna began to feel such intense pain that she needed to pace the floor back and forth. The word of Edna's labor had spread up and down the row of houses on Moxon's Yard. Frances asked a neighbor, Tommy Jacques, to head out in search of William as he made his way along High Street to let him know what had begun at home. William urgently quickened his steps and returned at about 3:00 p.m. from the pit. The midwife was not far behind him. Together they helped Edna to her feet and gently guided her through the kitchen and up the narrow red lino steps to the bedroom upstairs. Frances followed, helping her out of her frock and gently tucking her in. William placed a lamp by the bedside. The room was cold, and ice had formed on the windowpanes inside and out, making them opaque. William pulled the blind down and sat beside Edna on a wooden chair, holding her hand. Frances, meanwhile, made her way down to the kitchen to stoke the fire, heat water in the set pot, and prepare towels for the delivery. The midwife began to pull out her instruments from her sturdy leather bag, then lay them out on the dresser.

Day turned to night. Edna's labor pains were increasingly wrenching. As the midwife assessed the situation it was clear that she was concerned. Edna was having real difficulty, crying desperately in pain, thrashing and sweating. The baby was not emerging easily. The hours dragged by as Edna labored with little result and began losing both blood and stamina. As the weak morning sun began to rise to the east over Greasbro' Tops, the midwife sent William out to call for Dr. O'Connell, a mission that would channel his anxious pacing downstairs. Then the midwife put all her experience and skill to the difficult task. As Edna cried in pain, the midwife guided her to pant, pant, pant, then push, pant, pant, pant, then push some more. The crown of the baby's head was briefly visible, then receded, a pattern that repeated itself several times. The midwife held Edna's hand and wiped her brow, again coaxing her to push with all her might. Edna cried out some more and pushed again. Finally, after hours of exhausting, violent labor, the baby was born—and the reason for the particularly difficult labor became clear. Edna had given birth to a very large baby boy of ten pounds in weight. He appeared healthy despite everything and let out a great wail. The midwife quickly swaddled him to pass to Edna to hold, but she was weak and bleeding. She was barely conscious of her new son. Edna and William had already

54

chosen the name Harry if the baby was a boy. And here he was. Edna feebly held her son and marveled briefly at his tiny fingers. She had no more strength. The midwife gently cradled Harry in her arms, then handed the baby to Frances. Frances was elated at the birth of another grandson, but it was overshadowed by the fear she felt for her daughter-in-law. Edna had lost too much blood and been so wounded by the birth. She had chills, her heartbeat was too fast, and her body temperature was too high. She was in real danger of septicemia, the deadly blood poisoning infection. This could turn even more dangerously into Sepsis with its serious drop in blood pressure. It took the lives of thousands of women in Britain every year after they had survived the childbirth itself—and Rawmarsh had ones of the highest maternal mortality rates in the land.

Amid this William returned with Doctor O'Connell. He was elated at first at the sight of his baby son, but one look at Edna made it clear that she was in danger. His heart sank.

Doctor O'Connell recognized that Edna's body had been seriously wounded by the delivery. An ambulance would be needed—and Arthur Cooper next door readily agreed to sound the alarm. It was a Saturday morning, so several neighbors were home and had gathered outside of the house out of a mix of concern and curiosity. Dr. O'Connell accompanied the ambulance crew as they carefully carried Edna down the steep stairs of the house, then out and into the waiting ambulance to be taken and admitted to the Victorian-era Jessop Hospital for Women in Sheffield, twelve miles away. The first hospital built in Britain for women, it was the best hospital for tending to her badly torn body and crushed spirit. It was her only and best chance of survival. Dr. O'Connell then turned to the house to briefly comfort a clearly shaken William, then inspected baby Harry, declaring him healthy despite his large size and the ordeal he and his mother had been part of. The challenge now was to make a plan for the baby to suckle in his mother's absence. William's brother Leonard had also been waiting inside. Dr. O'Connell instructed him to go to the grocer and buy tins of evaporated milk. Frances stripped the bed of its bloodied sheets and took them out to the back yard to burn them. William gently cradled Harry in his arms, his elation at his son's arrival dampened by the crisis Edna faced.

Two days later on the Monday, with Edna in hospital in Sheffield, William went back to work. He had no choice but to return to work every day that God sent, whatever his personal circumstances. He had a home to keep up and now the doctor's and hospital's bills to be paid. There was no insurance to cover it, only whatever the family had paid in by sixpences at a time each week that was collected door-to-door by Mr. Lister on behalf of Dr. O'Connell. The bills would be a real burden for some time. Frances took charge of caring for her grandson until such time as his mother was well enough to return home from hospital, feeding Harry warmed evaporated milk from a baby bottle. It would have to do. This was the beginning of the strong bond that formed between grandmother and grandson. Mary Ellen Cooper from next door helped out, and baby Harry's aunts took turns helping Frances run the household and visiting Edna in hospital.

Edna made it through the worst with the care she received at Jessop. The doctors and sisters there were kind to her and carefully monitored her progress. She began to regain her strength. She also endured long, lonely hours of boredom and depression in the drafty ward of the imposing Gothic Revival building. Removed from the baby she had carried, she suffered a dispiriting sense of loss at not being able to be with him. Her milk came in painfully, with no chance to suckle her son. She heard he was thriving from William on the few visits he could make to her but was desperate to mother him herself. At least as her strength grew, she got to know other women recovering there. William and her sisters came to visit her when they could, which cheered her somewhat. William brought her daffodils—a sign that Spring was on its way—placing them in a jam jar at her bedside. She desperately wanted to come home.

At last her injuries healed and the danger of infection passed. When at last the day came that the doctors at Jessops declared Edna free from danger and healed enough to return home to William and the baby boy she had barely had a chance to hold in her arms, she was both hugely relieved. Though still weak, she returned home eager to see Harry. When she crossed the doorstep and stepped into the house, Frances stood in the front room cradling a sleeping Harry in her arms. Edna was thrilled to see her son. She also experienced a flash of resentment as she saw that grandmother and grandson were clearly comfortable with each other. The baby had thrived without her. She began to question whether she'd have the capacity to raise her own son. Motherhood was off to a difficult and confusing start.

With each day, little by little, Edna nurtured and got to know and bond with her son. She loved to touch his small fingers and stroke his soft cheeks. She stroked his small head with its dark hair. His light eyes sparkled, and he flashed big toothless smiles of unconditional love that brightened her spirits, and she returned the favor. "You're a sweet, cheeky little tyke," She cooed. She took pleasure in the visits of family to see the baby and her place at the center of it all. But she also struggled with waves of sadness—low feelings she couldn't understand but which sapped her spirit. Frances made sure to spend time with Edna and Harry each day to give mother time to rest, and to make sure Edna did not succumb to the low moods that were increasingly obvious to anyone who had known her before her childbirth ordeal.

On her first visit with Harry to see Dr. O'Connell upon her return home the doctor could see she was better but still weak, that she was putting on a brave face. He snuffed out his cigar as she entered his office, gently took Harry into his arms to admire him, unwrapping the baby's clothes to move about and inspect his limbs, and said, "Mrs. Bailey, you're taking such good care of this fine little boy. You're a wonderful mother." Edna beamed. Somehow Dr. O'Connell always made her feel better than when she had arrived. He knew enough to sit back and let her bask in this positive reinforcement for a few moments.

He then leaned forward toward Edna and spoke gently but firmly. "I think you understand the gravity of what you went through. You very nearly died giving birth to your beautiful son. I must put it to you, Mrs. Bailey: You must not have any more children. You could easily die if you do. Your body will not hold up. You must accept that in your situation Harry is enough. Please understand that."

He gently re-dressed and placed Harry back in her arms. Edna's face dropped down to look at her son. He flashed a toothless smile, but Edna did not reciprocate, her feelings lost in sorrow at Dr. O'Connell's counsel. Harry's face clouded, mirroring his mother's. As Edna looked up again at the doctor tears streamed down her cheeks. She wiped them away as best as she could with the back of her hand while fumbling for a handkerchief. Her lips quivered. She thought about William. What would he think? He loved children. It wasn't logical, but she felt she had failed him. She pulled Harry closer to her as the doctor sat quietly by as his words sunk in with her. She knew she could never go through what she had experienced giving birth again. Her hopes of a daughter someday were gone. Harry was to be her one and only child. She would need to accept that he was enough.

After sitting in silence with Dr. O'Connell for a few minutes, she felt ready to speak, if unsteadily. "Aye, I understand. You're right. I can't suffer through anything like that again. One child--It's not what William or I wanted—but we have Harry. He's beautiful." She smiled bravely down at him and held him closer. She loved him deeply. "He's enough."

And so it was that Harry was to be William's and Edna's only child. And that fact set him apart from countless more poor children from mining families.

A Controversial Christening

Harry's baptism was the important next order of business once Edna was home and stronger. The family prepared to gather together at St. Mary's Parish Church, the church Nanan's family, the Wilsons, had grown up in and around from cradle to grave for generations. There, in front of all the parishioners gathered, baby Harry would be welcomed into the Christian faith.

On the morning of Harry's Christening, William, dressed in his one and Sunday best suit, took extra care to polish his shoes. Edna straightened his tie for him after he buttoned the top of his starched dress shirt. She wore her Sunday best skirt, blouse, and a fashionable mauve cloche hat borrowed for the occasion from her sister Nellie. She dressed Harry in a white linen christening gown that William's sister—now Harry's Auntie Ethel—had made for his cousins Ernest and Jack Payne for their christenings only a few years before. With a chill still in the air Edna wrapped Harry up in an afghan she had knit of white yarn in the months leading up to his birth and placed a matching cap on his head, then the family made their way over to St. Mary's. Nanan Frances and Uncle Leonard had already made their way over to the church after quickly dropping in on William, Edna, and Harry at home to say good morning.

William and Edna, carrying Harry, entered the church. Harry's paternal aunts Ethel and Maggie were waiting inside. Upon seeing the new parents and their nephew, they presented a bag for Harry, called *the christening*, to William and Edna. It contained sugar for sweetness of life, salt (of the earth), a candle to light Harry's way in life, and bread so that he might never be hungry, plus a shiny new silver sixpence with King George V's silhouette on it for good luck. Edna and William then moved further into the church and settled into the pew beside Frances and Leonard for the service. William noticed his Auntie Florence, Frances's sister, sitting midway back and across the aisle. For as long as he remembered the two sisters always sat far apart in different pews from each other. She nodded her hellos to William and Edna with a slight smile before returning her gaze to the contents of the hymnal in her hands. Harry seemed to fix his gaze on the colourful stained-glass windows around him as Edna gently held his head in place. A few parishioners stopped by to greet the new parents and coo at Harry before taking their seats as the choir formed at the back to process toward the altar.

The first notes and trills to sound from the organ startled Harry a bit, but he returned to calm as Edna held him close and rocked him as the congregation stood and the choir made its way to the altar and during the singing of the first hymn. To everyone's relief, Harry mostly stared at the proceedings of the service or tucked his head into Edna's shoulder. By this point Edna had removed his little cap and mostly unwrapped his afghan.

The christening came later in the service. The Reverend Canon George Frederick Scovell bid the young parents approach the stone baptismal font to present the candidate. With all eyes on them Edna and William made their way to the font, the same one that had been used to baptize William, his siblings, Frances, her parents before her, and all her family for generations in Rawmarsh.

While William was tall at six feet in height, Canon Scovell was even taller, aristocratic in bearing and, clothed in his fine robes, especially imposing up close. William realized that he had been too preoccupied and nervous to even notice such details of ecclesiastical garments on his previous trip to the altar—on his wedding day four years before.

Scovell's patron in his appointment to the living at St. Mary's was the Lord Chancellor, the highest administrative officer serving the Crown. A graduate of Queen's College, Cambridge, Canon Scovell came from an aristocratic family which rose to prominence early in the 19th century. His forbear, George Scovell—later General Sir George Scovell—born a commoner of "low birth", was an exceptional linguist whose talents became clear while serving the Duke of Wellington during the Peninsula Wars between 1808-1814, against Napoleon Bonaparte. He developed highly effective communication, interception, and intelligence system and was credited as the chief code breaker of Napoleon's code. This gave the British the military intelligence to defeat Napoleon and the French Army, ultimately ending the wars that ravaged much of Europe.

With Edna, William, and baby Harry at the baptismal font and the congregation standing, Canon Scovell began the ages-old service from the *Book of Common Prayer:*

Celebrant	Blessed be God: Father, Son, and Holy Spirit.
People	And blessed be his kingdom, now and forever. Amen.
Celebrant	Bless the Lord who forgives all our sins;
People	His mercy endures forever.

The Celebrant then continued,

Celebrant	There is one Body and one Spirit;
People	There is one hope in God's call to us;
Celebrant	One Lord, one Faith, one Baptism;
People	One God and Father of all.
Celebrant	The Lord be with you.
People	And also with you.
Celebrant	Let us pray.

The service continued. As William and Edna stood up front by the font with all eyes on their backs in front of the congregation, the Baptism service seemed long. Harry began to fidget and whimper. Edna gently rocked him.

At last Canon Scovell began: "The candidate for holy baptism will now be presented."

Taking his cue, William cleared his throat nervously, then said, "I present Harry to receive the sacrament of Baptism."

From there the service did *not* continue quite as planned. Canon Scovell looked wide-eyed at the couple for a moment, then looked at the baby in Edna's arms before replying to William, "Come again? *Harry?* What's his *proper* name?"

William and Edna looked at each other in confusion for a moment, then William quietly replied, "His name is *Harry*."

Not content to take the baby's own father at his word, Canon Scovell replied in disbelief, "*Harry*? Not Henry? Not *Harold*? *Harry*? That's not a proper name!"

The sound of a pin dropping could have been heard at that moment as family members and all the congregation looked on, not sure what would happen next. Choir members, the organist, and the curates each craned their necks from their various positions seated at the altar to catch as good a glimpse as they could of the unexpected debate unfolding at the baptismal font.

William felt stifled and flush in his necktie, stiffly ironed shirt, and tightly buttoned collar. Heat began to make his neck prickly. It was intimidating enough to be up in front of the whole congregation, never mind having the Reverend Scovell question the name he and Edna had chosen for their son.

Someone broke the silence with an awkward, muffled cough. Edna held Harry a little tighter in one arm as she gently touched William's arm for a brief moment with her other hand. It calmed and re-assured him.

Then, for once ignoring all the expectations of social convention that he should not speak too boldly to his "betters," especially one so tall and imposing, William steadied his voice, stood taller, and spoke up firmly: "His name is *Harry*. We named him *Harry*. It's on his birth certificate. I present *Harry*!"

Reverend Scovell, who up until that moment had been rigid in attitude and his bearing, looked for a moment at the two parents and the baby Edna held tight in her arms. Perhaps he finally saw their vulnerability or admired how they stood up for themselves. As if a spell was broken, something in him softened and he nodded to them in a gentle and accepting fashion, then signaled the curate to pass the pitcher of holy water to him, filled the stone font, and got on with the christening.

He gently received Harry from Edna's arms, cradled him gently, looked into his small, alert face, then continued. When at last Reverend Scovell poured holy water on Harry's small head, Harry began to whimper as the cool water dribbled down his scalp.

"Harry," spoke the celebrant with extra emphasis, "I baptize you in the Name of the Father, and of the Son, and of the Holy Spirit. Amen."

He gently dabbed the water from Harry's scalp and, after all the ceremony was done, gently returned him back to Edna. The service continued as the parents and newly christened Harry returned to the pew beside Frances and Leonard.

William pulled out a crisply ironed white handkerchief, wiping the sweat from his brow. It had been a baptism unlike any other he had experienced. Edna, after so much standing, was tired and only too glad to no longer be at the center of the congregation's attention.

Harry was now baptized into the Christian faith, a new link in the family's life and history at St. Mary's. His baptism was the beginning of what was to become a formative relationship with the parish church that was to become a mainstay of his life in the years ahead.

A Young Family

If William was disappointed at the prospect of no more children, he didn't make it apparent to Edna. He took to fatherhood. And as Harry grew from infant to toddler, he benefited from the loving attention of two parents and a Nanan next door who truly enjoyed nurturing and playing with him. Nanan adored her newest grandchild and having him next door meant she got to see him daily. She was always glad to give Edna a break and take Harry for a toddle to the top of Moxon's Yard to watch all the activity on High Street or simply to "have a natter"—or chat—with neighbors. It was obvious to anyone within earshot when Nanan and neighboring Mrs. Charlesworth were deep in conversation. The latter had mostly lost her hearing and spoke loudly, so Nanan spoke loudly in return, ensuring that on those many occasions the neighbors up and down Moxon's Yard could hear every word, too.

There was more family close by. William had two older sisters: Ethel and her husband Joseph Payne lived just a five-minute walk away up High Street at Blythe Avenue with their sons Jack and Ernest. William's younger brother Leonard lived next door with Nanan.

On Edna's side, her eldest sister Nellie and her husband Harry Astbury lived in Rotherham; Her brother Harold, his wife Katherine, and their daughters Irene and Dorothy lived in nearby Ravenfield; And Edna's sister Elsie and brother-in-law Joe Wilson lived there too—above their fish & chip shop—with daughters "young" Elsie and Audrey. Edna also had three younger half-siblings: red-headed and kind-hearted Lucy, easy-going Rowland, and "our" Johnny, all of whom she adored, even if she disliked their mother Emily. Soon Harry would be able to play along with his cousins, so that being an only child wouldn't mean that he was without other children in his family life. Ever-present and overbearing in the lives of all his children and grandchildren was John Edward, the Dyson family patriarch. Often feared and in some ways loathed by his children, he was, despite his lack of kindness, also fiercely protective of his kin in unexpected ways. In short, the family was tight-knit and tended to look out for one another.

Edna was particularly fragile physically and emotionally in her first months with Harry. Each morning before he left for the pit William brought Edna a cup of tea in bed and made sure she knew she was cared for. She hadn't been the same since Harry's birth, overtaken by a deep melancholy that was most obvious in how she sat in bed with an expression of blank sadness, a feeling that was hard for her to shake each morning. He could see that she loved baby Harry and doted on him, but her former spark was missing. Edna's lovely soprano voice was heard less often. She had mostly stopped singing, except for nursery songs to Harry. Her mind often took her back to the darkest recesses of her childhood, replaying her sense of grief and abandonment about her mother's death, her feeling that "she never had a mother" once Lucy was gone. It was a painful time for her, one which filled her with confusion as she battled the demons of her childhood while trying with all she had left to embrace and love her new son.

Edna's world seemed to close in even more when construction equipment arrived in the field in front of the house a few yards across the way from Moxon's Yard: A new Regal Cinema was beginning to be built directly across from their front door. What had been open space between their front door and Downes' Butchers was now being filled with a large building that closed off the familiar view and its small patch of green. First the building site became a muddy pit as the cellar was dug, then its walls rose higher brick-by-brick, hemming in Moxon's Yard. Already struggling with bouts of sadness she couldn't explain, the new walls made her feel like her world was closing in on her.

The Regal was the talk of cinemagoers in Rawmarsh and the Rother Valley beyond, with promises that it would have the best sound system in the West Riding, "as good as any in London." It would have the newest technology, perfect for all the new "talking pictures" and musicals coming from London and faraway Hollywood in America, purpose built, not like the nearby retro-fitted-Methodist-chapel-turned Princess Cinema on High Street.

The Regal's new "cheap seats" entrance faced Moxon's Yard directly across from the Baileys' front door. There would be little privacy for the families living there as people in search of something of the wider world and the exotic queued at the ticket window right across from their front doors. While Edna enjoyed going to the cinema, the idea of one so close to the front of their home meant there would be a regular audience just outside the Bailey home for their daily activities of doing their best to get on with their lives.

When at last the cinema opened in October 1932, Edna and William were among the first patrons, with Edna's sister Elsie and brother-in-law Joe riding over from Ravenfield after encouraging Edna to join them to take a break from her daily cares and Nanan happily agreeing to watch an active two-and-a half-year-old Harry.

When the couples paid for their seats at the stalls entrance across from Edna's and William's front door, they then stepped into a world entirely removed from the one they knew all too well just outside the new cinema's walls: Like a fine theatre in Sheffield or London, the cinema boasted an elegant, velvet-curtained proscenium arch to frame the black-and-gold-tabbed screen, and fine plaster work painted in fashionable tones of primrose, vermillion, red, and ivory. Edna, who had only seen the building when it was a disheveled building site, was in awe. It brought something of the exotic to life—and the first film shown, *Just Imagine*, a Maureen O'Sullivan science fiction musical set in a futuristic 1980s New York full of 250-storey buildings, suspension bridges, and elevated roads full of sleek flying vehicles —was worlds removed from the grit and wholly unglamorous reality of scrubbing, mending, and barely managing to get by on Moxon's Yard. The modern sound system provided a film-watching experience like none the couples had experienced before. The Regal provided a much-welcomed breath of fresh air into Edna's life, despite her earlier worries and misgivings during its construction.

"God, Bring me Some Work!"

1931-1934

As the aftershocks of the 1929 Wall Street crash in the United States took hold in Britain in 1930, economies around the world collapsed with tragic consequences. Millions lost jobs as nations enacted protectionist trade policies and older industries like mining were particularly battered. The British economy—so dependent on world trade—was deeply impacted. Redundancies and reduced working days meant miners were without livelihoods for weeks—and frequently months—at a time. William was no more spared than most miners in the West Riding. Desperation throughout Yorkshire was immense as work and already eroded wages from the failed 1926 strike fell further and then disappeared. William was among the thousands upon thousands upon thousands of British miners who found themselves without work, or with reduced work hours, thus no or lower wages one week to the next.

The government appeared indifferent at best to their plight and seemingly incapable of doing anything to alleviate the financial disaster bringing collapse especially hard to the region's economy. The situation dragged from 1930 to 1931 to 1932 to 1933 to 1934—with little or no relief in sight. While other parts of the country began to recover and flourish as new jobs grew in light manufacturing in the Midlands and further south toward London, in these painful years, large parts of Yorkshire, the industrial north, Wales, and Scotland floundered catastrophically. One sign: The maternal and infant mortality rate in Rawmarsh rose to be among the highest in the nation as poor nutrition and other hardships affected women's lives as they frequently went with less food to make sure their husbands and children had more.

Harry was now aware enough at four years old to know that his dad's regular presence at home during many weeks and months over those years were not happy days for his *Dada*. Sometimes William sat in his chair in the front room staring blankly at something Harry could not see. Other days he heard his dad rise at 4:00 a.m., dressed for work down the pit, only to see him return home a few hours later unsuccessful in his efforts to earn a day's wages. On those painful days

Edna often brought Harry next door to visit his Nanan for a biscuit when she saw William's expression that mixed misery and humiliation as he walked, stooped over, into the house, agonizing over how he could afford to keep the roof over their heads or hold his head up.

While Nanan read to and played with Harry for hours at a time next door, William suffered as dread and fear gripped him mind, body, and spirit. Sometimes, to cope, he went to the family allotment on Rockliffe Road to tend to growing carrots, cabbage, green beans, and Brussel sprouts. It was the one place where he experienced the pleasure of seeing something thrive and where he could count on the company of other men to talk to who faced the same challenges.

He also made his way to the Star Inn pub for the occasional pint of ale and the camaraderie and comfort of the pub full of friends and acquaintances alike. So many men were trapped in the same situation, all trying to cope in their own ways. If misery loved company, it was also a place where the men could commiserate, lift each other's spirits. Sometimes it was talk of the Doncaster and Grand National horse races, others about the dog races, other times about what the government or the union were or weren't doing to help them and their families.

Sometimes the neighbors gathered broke into a singsong to lift their collective spirits. At home, Edna did her best to live the words of the song everyone sang during the Great War: *"Pack up your troubles in your old kit bag, and smile, boys, smile…"* Despair was an all-too-frequent reality in their lives, especially on the mornings when the various bill collectors came by and William and Edna didn't have enough to satisfy them all. It was Edna's job to negotiate a partial payment or none on any given week as the rent man, insurance man, gas man, doctor's office, and so many others came by to collect. William stayed clear of these visits, sometimes moving to the kitchen or upstairs rather than being seen. It was painful to him to be unable to provide for these most basic of needs for his family, to see Edna patching and darning their increasingly threadbare clothes.

Sometimes William went to the newly opened Regal for a few hours to watch the newsreels and feature film. It was a diversion. If far off America started the troubles that led to a collapsed economy in Rawmarsh, its Hollywood films could also be a source of entertainment. The Regal offered warmth—the chance to pack up one's troubles if only for a few hours.

Day upon day, month upon month, year blending into new year, William went from business to business, pit to pit, pleading for work, any work, but was one of many miners doing the same. The supply of men desperate to do anything to earn anything to support their struggling families far outstripped demand for their labor. Sometimes he wanted nothing more than to stay in bed and hide from the confines of his situation. He imagined his family better off if he died. The mounting cost of days, weeks, then months of little or no work was that the Baileys, like almost every other one else they knew, was on or crossed the brink of disaster—in debt, struggling to pay what they increasingly owed to creditors, cutting food purchases at the Co-Op further, being unable to pay for healthcare, scraping pennies together to keep the gas on for cooking and light, mending and darning what had already been mended and darned, sending their children into the shops to ask the shopkeepers for any broken biscuits they could sell at a reduced price, and—before being chased off by mine owners—scouring and scaling the filthy, perilously high slag heaps that closed in around them in hopes of finding coal pieces to warm the house. Without work in the mines the concessionary coal deliveries to mining families stopped too. Newspaper was a prized commodity not just for news but for heating homes and stuffing into the bottom of shoes and boots with holes in them to extend their wear and absorb leaks. On more than one occasion, when all else was scarce, books, family Bibles, pianos, and other home furniture became kindling and fuel for the fire of thousands of homes in the Rother Valley. It was a place forsaken.

As a proud Yorkshireman and miner, William's self-respect and identity were tied to his ability to work and to his ability to provide for his wife and child. And on one bitterly cold winter morning after another Harry heard his dad rise early and dress to head out in search of a day's work. William, with a snap tin of bread and drippings in hand and a flask of water to drink, headed to Aldwarke Main Colliery, then to Roundwood, New Stubbin, then Warren Vale, to mines large and small in the valley, only to be turned away at the gates of each because there was no work. Morning after morning it happened. On one morning, William went out on a bitterly cold winter morning to see if he could get work at Aldwarke, only to be turned away. He continued walking miles onto the next, then the next colliery, only to be turned away again and again. Unable to pay the fare for the warmth, cover, and comfort of the trackless tram, he trudged with increasing hunger, stinging frost-bitten toes, and thirst throughout the district—with no success finding work. Chilled to the bone, dead tired, stung by the pin-and-needles of frostbite on his ears and by his feelings of impotence in being unable to provide for his family, he had walked over twenty miles in icy rain that day in search of work before he returned home with nothing to show for this exhausting effort.

Edna was in the front room coaxing as much heat in the fire as possible with old dried tea and newspaper for fuel when William arrived home. Harry had just returned from a visit to Nanan's next door and sat quietly on a small wooden chair beside her looking through the nursery rhymes book she had borrowed for him from the warm, cozy Carnegie Library in Parkgate earlier in the day. William threw the door open, close to hypothermia, then stepped in with the heavy weight of defeat, his coat shoulders encrusted with ice, his clothes from head to foot all but frozen stiff from rain that had turned to ice. Edna was shocked at the sight of her ice-covered husband. She helped him remove his coat and led him to his chair to remove his boots. His fingers, feet, and ears stung. He could scarcely look her in the eyes. Involuntarily, he cried out as plaintively as a proud Yorkshireman could, "God, give me some work!", then burst into tears and buried his face in his hands as his whole frame shook as he sobbed.

At first Edna froze. She had never seen William cry before. Then she tried to comfort him. William couldn't look at her. His body shook as he struggled to stop the tears. "We'll all be in bloody Alma Road before long—separated from one another" he cried out, referring to the dreaded Victorian-era workhouse in Rotherham that for generations had struck fear into the hearts of the working-class people in the area. The prospect of losing what little they had—most of all their self-respect—was overwhelming. Just then, Harry, who had minutes before closed his book to observe his dada, quietly dropped from his chair onto the floor and walked over to William. He gently touched his dada's knee with his small hand, then, turned his head to one side to peer up into William's hands-covered faced, trying to catch his eyes. In his small voice he consolingly said, "Dada, don't cry…It will be all right. I love you!"

86

William had not noticed Harry was in the room before then, assuming he'd be at Nanan's next door. The gentle touch of Harry's small warm hand on his knee comforted him and the compassion in Harry's kind little voice as he spoke to his beloved protector warmed him.

Choking back his tears, William became suddenly quiet, his body shuddering a little less. He removed his hands from his face, wiped his eyes and nose with a carefully pressed handkerchief Edna offered him, then gazed down at his small son, looking deeply into Harry's eyes. Harry met his stare with a steadiness, warmth, and compassion in his small face that astonished William.

William gazed lovingly at Harry, touched his dark, soft hair, then gently lifted his son onto his knees and hugged him closely. Harry burrowed his head into his dada's chest, listening to his strongly beating heart. Father and son clung to each other quietly for several minutes without another word between them. Edna slipped into the kitchen to make William a cup of tea.

In time William's body and spirit warmed up. Harry's unconditional love for his father had been what he needed on that desperate, dark day. There would be many more days and months of no or too little work for William and too little money for the family. There would also be days when, after getting some work, the pay was less for the same production than it had been a week or month before. Somehow William and Edna found the emotional and physical stamina to keep going despite the suffering they endured. And Harry, as young as he was, strengthened them with his unconditional love and their awakening to the promise they saw within him.

Hiding from the Police

1934

"Mummy!?" Harry asked Edna as he stood outside in the yard watching Edna vigorously doing her outdoor cleaning and preparing to scrub, then color the front step with a white strip with donkey stone one morning, "Why do you call donkey stone *donkey stone*? Is it because donkeys have white bellies and white tips on their noses like the ones we saw at the seaside at Scarborough?" It was a serious question for Harry, whose state of curiosity was constant. Edna took time for scrubbing hard against the soot and grime on hands and knees, paused to look up at Harry, thought for a few moments about the donkeys they saw at the seaside on a day trip there, then replied, "I don't know son. I've never really thought about it. Your guess is as good as any my lamb!"

"Well," said Harry with a pensive and serious tone, "Nanan says it's because the stone comes from a factory on a wharf called Donkey Wharf," continued Harry, "But that seems daft…I think it's because of donkeys' white bellies."

Edna, amused, was just thinking more about Harry's theory about the origin of the scouring block's name when the conversation was interrupted by the loud *Vroom, vroom, vroom* of a motorbike with sidecar turning into Moxon's Yard. It approached them slowly, driven by a man in uniform. Edna quickly saw that it was her brother-in-law Joe Wilson's motorbike—and, for some reason in that moment, a sight and sound that struck fear in Harry's heart.

Taking one look at the approaching motorbike, Harry burst into tears and fled to Nanan's house, quickly opening her door and slamming it behind himself.

Uncle Joe turned off the motor, then dismounted from his motorbike and approached Edna saying with a chuckle, "What's the matter with the little tyke then?"

"I don't know, but he doesn't like the sight or sound of you, Joe Wilson!" Edna replied laughing. "We'd best ask him!" She caught sight of the curtain at Nanan's parted to one side of the window and Nanan and Harry peering out of it, with an expression of dread on Harry's face.

Edna walked next door to Nanan's to call after Harry to come and say hello to his uncle. Frances opened the door enough to speak with Edna. "He's having none of it," she said protectively and as Harry hid behind her skirt inside.

"Come Harry," beckoned Edna.

"No, I won't!" said Harry with more than a little fear mixed with resolve in his voice.

"Whatever is the matter, then?" Edna replied to him.

"Why am I in trouble?" Harry asked

"In trouble?" replied Nanan. "Who says you're in trouble, dove?"

His voice shaking. "Uncle Joe's come to arrest me! Am I in trouble with the police?"

"Arrest you?" said Edna. "Your Uncle Joe? He's not a policeman!"

"Then why does he have a motorbike and wear that uniform?" Harry cried out.

"Oh lad!" Edna replied, not able to help laughing. "Your uncle works for the trackless company! He's wearing his conductor's uniform!" Harry was unconvinced.

"If he works for the trackless, then why does he need a motorbike?" Harry said, his voice still quavering, his trust in this information low.

"Come then Harry," said Uncle Joe gently, approaching Nanan's door, "Tha's being a silly 'un! I ride my motorbike because I have the first trackless run every day even before the sun rises—long before you're awake—and as such there's no trackless to collect *me* to go to work, is there?!" He winked at Harry with a warm smile and a friendly laugh.

Harry wasn't sure whether to believe his uncle or not.

"Our young Harry must have a guilty conscience!" Edna continued, trying to make light of Harry's fears that Uncle Joe was the police, there to arrest him and take him away to jail. Harry was puzzled, not knowing what that meant.

"Go on, Harry," said Nanan gently, "You're not in trouble with the police. You're a good lad—and your Uncle Joe just popped 'round to bring something to your mother from your Auntie Elsie. I wager if you come outside, he'll let you climb on his motorbike, maybe even give you a ride in his side car to Parkgate and back!" Harry wasn't so sure.

"Would you like that then?" Said Edna.

Harry looked out warily from behind Nanan, not sure whether to believe the grownups around him or not.

"Look here, Harry," said Uncle Joe, "I wager there's thre'ppence behind your ear if you let me take a look!"

Harry stepped outside again tentatively, not sure whether to believe his uncle or not, but eager to find out if there was, in fact, thre'ppence behind his ear. He felt behind both ears, feeling no coins.

"There's not thre'ppence behind my ears!" he protested.

"Ah, young tyke, but there is," replied Uncle Joe. "Come let me show you."

And with that, he gently approached Harry, knelt on one knee at Nana's step, felt behind Harry's right ear, then pulled a shiny thre'ppence coin from behind it and showed it to Harry, who beamed with excitement.

"Look at that, son!" beamed Edna. "How did your Uncle Joe ever find thre'ppence then?"

Harry was mystified and excited about it. He studied the coin closely, as he had never held one before, admiring King

George's silhouette on one side and acorns and oak leaves on the other.

"Harry, now you have money in your pocket we must take a ride with my motorbike to Parkgate and get you something special at the bakery!"

Harry liked the idea of a visit to the bakery. He and Edna had passed by it many times on their way to and from the Carnegie Library, passing window displays full of tempting baked goods—cakes, tarts, cream-filled scones, and ginger folk with sultana buttons. They had looked in the windows but never stopped into the bakery before. It was a luxury that was not within their means.

"What do you think, then, Harry?" said Nanan with a question that was more like an encouragement.

With the promise of the bakery, Harry turned to Edna, saying, "Mummy, may I?"

"If your Uncle Joe is willing to take you, then aye!" Edna replied.

Harry looked shyly at Uncle Joe, then said, "I'd like to go with you to Parkgate—as long as you don't take me to the police."

Uncle Joe laughed, "Go on then Harry, I'm not taking you to the police young tyke—unless you've been robbing banks?!"

With great seriousness, Harry shook his head no, he had not been robbing banks. With that, he stepped closer toward Uncle Joe, who helped him step into the side car of his motorbike. Then Uncle Joe climbed onto the motorbike, fired up the engine, and, as it putt-putt-puttered slowly, he turned the motorbike and sidecar around to face High Street.

Edna and Nanan watched and waved from their doorsteps and Harry looked smiling back and waved, trusting that Uncle Joe wasn't the police and he wasn't going to jail. With Harry at his side, Uncle Joe slowly made his way to Parkgate.

"Well, I don't know what gets into his mind sometimes," said Edna to Nanan once the motorbike was out of sight. "Wherever did he get the idea that Joe was the police and he was in trouble?" She laughed.

"He has such an active imagination. It's his brightness. His young mind is always on the go." replied Nanan. "I wager he and Joe will become the best of chums by the end of this ride."

"Aye," replied Edna as she dipped her scrub brush into a pail of water to continue what she had begun before all the fuss, "That would be a good thing." The two women smiled at each other, then went in the direction of their respective doorsteps to get back to their work.

When Harry and Uncle Joe *vroom-vroom*ed back down Moxon's Yard 40 minutes later, Harry was laughing, smiling, and waving a gingerbread man—minus one of its legs already eaten—high above his head to show Edna. One thing was certain: Uncle Joe was now his friend and he looked forward to many more chances to ride around Rawmarsh in his uncle's side car—with hopefully many more stops at the bakery.

Blackpool Rock

1936

Dale Road School was a short distance from Moxon's Yard—just down Stocks Lane, past Walker Scales' butcher shop, then up past a few houses to Dale Road and the school itself. At five years old, Harry was now ready to enter the first form, having spent a year at St. Mary's Infants School. From the start, Harry was in a league of his own, ahead of the other children his age in reading and writing. He was reading at home by three years old and Edna and Nanan had encouraged him in writing, too. He was able to write all his letters and numbers.

Still, there was plenty more to learn, and when he started at his new school, he was hungry for every lesson his teachers delivered. He was frequently called on to read aloud in class—and it was soon clear to the teachers that he needed more to do to feed his voracious appetite for learning.

School was not all about lessons. There were many other things Harry and all the children needed to learn—like getting along with each other and minding what the teachers had to say.

Mr. Cater, the head teacher, made certain that his students paid attention and followed the school rules. The children called him "Blackpool Rock" in an ironic twist because he carried a thick, shiny black cane similar in diameter and appearance to the much-enjoyed "cane" sweets from the seaside resort. One sight of Mr. Cater's cane was typically enough to strike fear and spur his students into hushed obedience. He had no qualms about using it to strike the children on their hands or backsides if they did not do as they were told.

Each morning at school followed a similar routine: Mr. Cater entered the room with rigid formality and placed his black cane on his desk at the front of the room. With that gesture, all fell silent. He then greeted the boys and girls with, "Good morning children!" This was their cue to relax a bit and reply in sing-song unison, "Good morning Mr. Cater!" The children then began their lessons.

The teachers at Dale Road were mostly a caring team. Many were "spinsters", unmarried women whose fiancés had died in the brutality of the Great War or who hadn't married because of the tragic shortage of young men after the war. Most of the teachers also understood that the poor Rawmarsh children they taught had a short window for learning in their lives and needed to be able to at least read, write, and do maths to a degree of proficiency and be ready to leave school by 14 or 15 to begin working.

For Harry, one thing became clear: His teachers quickly recognized something exceptional about his intellect and hunger for learning. They did what they could to give him more to feed his quick mind, making sure he had books and magazines to read to feed his curious mind.

Edna was pleased as punch when she ran into one of Harry's teachers, Miss Allott, at a shop on Stocks Lane one afternoon. "Mrs. Bailey, your Harry is a highly intelligent boy. Whatever you are doing at home, let's not waste his intelligence. We'll do what we can to keep him interested in his lessons at school. I know he is particularly drawn to books about animals. I'm reading *The Wind in the Willows* to the class now. He seems particularly fond of it. Please promise me that you'll take him to the Carnegie Library to get books that interest him. That's what Mr. Carnegie had in mind when he funded his libraries—a place for children like Harry to make something more of themselves."

"Aye," replied Edna with quiet, blushing pride. "He seems to have been learning from almost the moment he was born. I do my best to keep up with him on that score. He loves to read whatever he can get his hands on…even *The Daily Mirror*," she said, referring to the tabloid popular with Labour households.

"Might I also suggest *The Illustrated London News*, Mrs. Bailey," replied Miss Allott. "It will give him a window on the wider world. The Carnegie will have it—and the photographs are quite captivating. Harry really does stand out as one of the most exceptional children I've taught. It's a gift—and it would be a pity not to cultivate his intellectual curiosity."

Edna, who had been feeling the discomfort of the damp chill before running into Miss Allot, felt a warmth of pride now throughout her frame as she replied, "Aye, ta, then—

thank you—Miss Allott. We'll look for it next time we're at the Carnegie. Harry looks forward to going there and looking at all the books. I usually bring my knitting to give him plenty of time in the stacks there."

The two women nodded their good-byes and continued their shopping. That short exchange gave Edna a much-needed boost to her spirits as she and William went through the daily slog of their lives. Harry was something special—a son to be proud of. She was grateful that Harry's teachers saw promise in him.

♦ ♦ ♦

As the early years of school progressed, Harry made friends. He enjoyed going to school with Derek and Alan Cooper from next door and with his cousins Jack and Ernest from Dale Road. John Turner from church was another good friend—and the Baileys and Turner parents frequently met in the evenings at the Star Inn for a drink and a singsong while the boys played together on Moxon's Yard under Nanan's caring, watchful eye.

An important part of Harry's growth and education was Rawmarsh itself—the streetscapes, shops, and what he experienced as he walked to and from school each day—in the morning, back home for lunch, back to school again, then home. He encountered all manner of people, getting to know the shopkeepers and tradesmen along the way. The daily interactions in his community life helped him grow. Many mornings he waved hello to Cufty Evans, who worked for the local council and swept the streets tidy despite having only one arm—the loss of the other was a casualty of the Great War.

Other days Harry and his friends watched as Jockey G, the wiry, small-framed rag and bone man, rode from door to door with his old horse and cart to haul away what people didn't want—or to deliver furniture and other large home items from one place to another. The boys amazed at the small man's strength as he single-handedly hoisted furniture and other bulky, heavy items onto his cart. And each day, as they headed to and from school, the boys stopped by Scales's Butchers to pat the pigs in the pen on their snouts. On other occasions, the boys hastened by as they heard the plaintive squeals of a pig being slaughtered for the pork roast, chops, bacon, and pork pies that would soon feed the neighborhood.

Every day the high-pitched whirring and low rumblings of the trackless coming and going, making the turn at High Street and Stocks Lane at the corner by Ward's greengrocer on its way to and from Rotherham and Mexborough meant that there was a wider world beyond the old, narrow medieval streets and rows of narrow houses that reflected Rawmarsh's rapid 19th century industrial growth. Harry liked to guess at what individual plans set so many people in motion each day. He looked forward to occasional trackless rides with Edna and William, to explore places beyond the environs of High Street and Stocks Lane that he knew best. Each ride brought new sights and sounds—from advertisements for Bovril meat extract, Sun Laundry Flakes, and Players Cigarettes that were plastered on buildings to reading the news posted on boards outside the newsagents along the way—to cricket headlines or other news in a newspaper being read by a passenger in front of him, Harry was hungry to learn and curious about the world around him.

Miss Shirley Temple

1936

"Nanan!" Harry announced one day, "I am going to marry Shirley Temple!" He had just seen the pint-sized, curly-topped American screen sensation in *The Little Colonel* with Elsie and Irene at the Regal.

"That's lovely, Harry," said Nanan with a smile. "You know she lives a very long way away in America?!"

"America!" replied Harry, "Do you think I can ride a horse there like a cowboy?"

"Oh no, dear," said Nanan with a gentle laugh, "You must take a ship to America and that takes many days at sea. Then you probably need to take a train."

"Oh, but I will marry her!" said Harry after thinking about this geographical obstacle for a few minutes. "Maybe I can take an aeroplane to meet her?" He inquired.

"An aeroplane to America? Now that's an idea!" replied Nanan. "I don't know of any aeroplanes to America here, maybe from London 'though."

"But dada says I could be like Charles Lindbergh and fly there. Who is Charles Lindbergh?"

"Oh—he is a pilot and the first one to fly all by himself from America to France. That was a good eight years ago or so!" said Nanan.

"Do you think he knows Shirley Temple?" asked Harry, thinking about this for a few moments, "Maybe he could fly me over to America to meet her!"

"Or perhaps Beryl Markham could take you!" replied Nanan, thinking of the first pilot to fly solo successfully from East to West across the Atlantic to Nova Scotia. "Keep dreaming, Harry, and perhaps one day you will travel to California and meet Shirley Temple. She's a lovely lass. She'd be a fine addition to our family!" Said Nanan.

"Will you take me back to see *The Little Colonel* again?" asked Harry. "I'd like to see her dance and sing again, especially since I'm going to marry her."

"Aye, Harry, I'll take you. I'd like to see my future granddaughter-in-law!"

Harry beamed with joy, hugged Nanan, then flew on home. Nanan laughed at the idea that Harry was in love with a film star—and an American one at that.

True to her word, Nanan brought Harry to the next Saturday matinee at the Regal. Afterward, she promised to take Harry to the next Shirley Temple film that came to Rawmarsh. And so, Harry and his Nanan made it a habit to see the young curly-topped American girl's films, often joined by cousins Irene, Elsie, Audrey, and Dorothy, all of whom admired little Miss Temple's singing, dancing, and curly-topped head.

Long Live the King

1936

Prince Edward, affectionately known as "David" to people across Britain and the empire, had served in the Great War with distinction. Dashing and exuding youthful vitality at 41, to many he embodied a refreshing modernity that was lacking in his father, King George V. As the nation mourned the death of King George in January 1936, there was yet a sense that change was in the air with his modern-thinking, debonair heir. Edward flew his own airplane after all.

At school, Harry and his classmates experienced the change as portraits of the future king were hung in their classrooms, even though his coronation was still to take place. At church, the year started with prayers for the health of the soon-to-be crowned new king.

But the hopes that came with the upcoming coronation of Edward were soon dashed. His interest in an American divorcee, Wallis Simpson, soon became his obsession and the subject of gossip in high society, government, and the Church of England. The latter two powers were united in opposing his goal of marrying "Mrs. Simpson" and insisted that it would be impossible for Edward to have what he wanted, which was the crown and Wallis Simpson as his queen and consort.

Yet in mining families, the growing scandal of the new king's love for an American divorcé was almost a foreign affair and largely unknown to them even as late as November 1936. In that month he visited Welsh mining communities and witnessed a malnourished, poorly clothed, struggling population of mining families firsthand. He solemnly remarked to them that, "Something must be done" and reassured residents in a run-down housing estate that "You can be assured that all that I can do for you I will." His remarks lifted the spirits of mining families not only in Wales but in the Rother Valley, too.

But in government and church leadership, Edward's social commentary was seen as taking an ill-considered foray into political territory off-limits to the royal family.

William, Edna, and everyone they knew saw the future king with affection for him. "He's such a handsome man—

and he cares about families like ours," Edna and Emily Cooper agreed as they washed the windows of their adjacent homes one morning. William, Leonard, and Frank Pickering agreed that Edward was a breath of fresh air, a sign of hope that something, in fact, would be done to alleviate the hardships of their lives. At last the monarchy was a voice for them and their struggles.

But soon the hope in and belief that Edward had genuine concern for their plight came crashing down in the pit towns of Britain. Newspaper proprietors and Buckingham Palace had for months ensured that most people in Britain knew nothing of the scandal of the king showering his mistress Mrs. Simpson with jewels, wining and dining her at home and abroad while she was still married, then divorced, and pouring vastly more of his attention on her than on affairs of state as his coronation drew near. Far more was known in the press abroad about their relationship and opposition to it than all but a tiny minority of Britons did. The Edward and Mrs. Simpson affair was the focal point of gossip in far-off New York. Any news of it coming into Britain was censored, literally by cutting the news out of foreign newspapers coming into the country.

Finally, after months of suppressed news on the matter, the critical remarks of a bishop upbraiding Edward for not being a regular churchgoer gave the press the excuse they were looking for to break their silence. The scandal broke out in newspapers across the land. The Establishment and mainstream newspapers strongly opposed the king marrying a now-divorced Mrs. Simpson and making her "Queen Wallis." In working class newspapers and on Moxon's Yard and in most working-class communities, most people thought it would be fine for Edward to marry "The woman I love."

But by December, while the normal focus of everyone's attention was Advent and the coming of Christmas, instead cinema newsreels focused on the sensationalism of what would happen next. Newsagents ran out of copies of the papers that now carried every available morsel of news on the scandal. Edward abdicated, giving up the crown for Wallis Simpson. Reluctantly, the painfully shy Duke of York, Edward's younger brother Albert, known as "Bertie," assumed the throne, the dutiful new king would take the crown as King George VI and his wife would be Queen Elizabeth. Their two young daughters, the Princesses Elizabeth and

Margaret Rose, became the "heir and a spare." Curly-haired young Elizabeth was to be second in line to the throne.

In mining families, the sense of Edward's betrayal of them mounted. William, Edna, and everyone they knew had placed high hopes in him as their champion, only to discover that the words they took to heart that "Something must be done" a month before were shallow and meaningless.

"We're better off without him," William declared angrily to Edna upon reading the news of Edward's abdication. Edna agreed with a deep sense of sadness that nothing would be done.

Harry witnessed and absorbed the shock and anger growing in the adults around him, as it became increasingly clear that their hopes in Edward had been misplaced. It was painful, even humiliating to mining families. Harry had never seen his dada quite so angry. The national drama bore painfully into the hopes of mining families across the country.

At school and at church, portraits of and prayer for "the king" Edward were quickly replaced to instead focus on Prince Albert, now King George VI, Queen Elizabeth,

Princess Elizabeth, Princess Margaret-Rose, "...and all the royal family."

Uncle Zach's Pilgrimage

1937

Each Spring, Ascension Day marked the 40 days since Easter, and celebrated the ascension of Jesus to Heaven. It was a day of festivities along the High Street: Robed clergy and parishioners from evangelical "Nonconformist" Congregationalist, Methodist, Adventist, Baptist, and Presbyterian churches and chapels vied to outdo each other each year with the size of their processions and the creativity of their colourful floats depicting Biblical stories. Youth group members dressed as characters like David, Job, Jesus, Mary, and Joseph among many. They carried banners and sang hymns. St. Mary's, the "Established" Anglican church, did not participate, but the lively procession route passed right by its gates and past Moxon's Yard.

Since Ascension Day was a holiday, the pits, shops, schools, and pubs closed. The sky, even if not clear, somehow seemed less smoggy. Everyone took the opportunity to enjoy what would hopefully be fine spring weather.

For the Baileys, Ascension Day also meant a family reunion: The annual visit of Uncle Zach—or Zachariah Bailey—from Shropshire. Uncle Zach was Nanan's brother-in-law and uncle to William and his siblings Maggie, Ethel, and Leonard. He was great uncle to Harry and cousins Ernest and Jack Payne and Dennis Marshall. He made his annual pilgrimage to exchange Bailey family news, calling in on his brother's widow. The extended Shropshire Bailey family had never met Nanan: She had scarcely ever left Rawmarsh and the Shropshire Baileys—except her husband William and Zach—had stayed close to home, too.

Zach Bailey, like Frances's beloved husband William, hailed from the village of Dawley, Shropshire—close to Shrewsbury and "in view of the Wrekin"—the landmark 1,300-foot hill in the east of the county that was formed in large part by volcanic rocks.

Uncle Zach fascinated Harry. Now in his 60s, he wore a large black brimmed hat and all-black attire that harkened back to the Victorian era. To Harry he seemed like a relic from a long-gone time. Most striking of all was his thick, distinct

Shropshire accent and dialect—one rarely heard beyond Dawley, never mind miles away in Rawmarsh.

Uncle Zach's arrival in Rawmarsh happened with great reliability each year; he sent a short letter to Nanan a few weeks ahead announcing his plans to visit. He had started making the visits when he was a young man and his brother William had moved to and stayed in Rawmarsh after marrying Frances.

Everyone knew that if it was Ascension Day, Uncle Zach would soon amble down to the end of Moxon's Yard to call on Nanan and his nephews and nieces, arriving before the procession of floats made its way past. Harry, Jack, and Ernest hung around at the top of Moxon's Yard and High Street watching the processions and with an eye open for the distinctive tall figure dressed in black to make his way up Rawmarsh Hill toward them.

Upon arrival at Nanan's, Uncle Zach reliably inquired after her health with a distinctive Shropshire "*Ow bist?*"—or "How are you?" Before stepping inside he removed his big black hat, revealing a full head of thick gray hair, wiped his brow, fanned his face with his hat, and declared, "I'm sweating cobs in this warm weather."

Nanan planned ahead, preparing a special tea for him, baking tarts, and putting on ham, cheese, and chutney. She sent either Harry or Derek to the Earl Grey the day before Ascension Day to pick up a few extra bottles of Tenant's India Pale Ale, her own daily favorite.

Zach's presence was a welcome event for Nanan each year. She saw many resemblances in him to her late husband. They were cut from the same cloth after all.

Conversing with Uncle Zach required an annual tuning of the ears to understand his accent and pronunciation of everyday words. He liked to have a good "chin wag" with his sister-in-law and he took great interest in Harry's growth. "Ow bist thee owd jockey?" he'd ask his great nephew in a booming voice. "That means 'How are you young lad?'" Nanan would translate.

"Surree! Look at how thou hast grown!" Uncle Zach declared as he took the measure of his young relations.

"I canna imagine how your mother and father keep up wi' ye! It's a wonder, inna?" Harry blushed and moved to stand behind Nanan's chair. He didn't fear Uncle Zach; He was simply somewhat taken aback by his directness and confusing expressions.

"Listen up then, owd jockey, let me tell you this," Zach declared to Harry, "If you can see the Wrekin then rain is coming. If you *canna* see the Wrekin, it's already raining!" Harry smiled broadly.

Harry made a point of lingering nearby to listen to the family news. He knew that if Nanan had put on a spread for tea and baked for Uncle Zach, she had been sure to make enough for him, too.

Feast Week: Fair Folk and the Travellers Come to Rawmarsh

1937

"Mum, mum—come quick!" Harry shouted with excitement as he skipped over the front step and reeled into the house. "Up at the top—the fair folk are here! The traction engines are on their way up High Street!"

With that, Harry spun on his heels again, racing back out the door toward the Coopers' front door. He rapped the door quickly. Mary Ellen Cooper soon answered, holding a tea towel in one hand as she wiped off the remains of flour on her hands and the doorknob. "The big traction engine is coming! The fair is here! Can Alan, Derek, and Edgar come see?" Harry asked.

"Aye, young Harry," said Mary Ellen, smiling gently. She turned, headed to the kitchen, and called up the stairs, "Here, lads, come quick! Harry's at the door and is heading to see the fair folk arrive. Look sharp!"

With that, Edgar first, followed by Alan and Derek, clamored down the narrow, red lino steps to the kitchen and then up to the front door to join up with Harry. Mary Ellen watches as the four boys took off up Moxon's Yard to the corner next to catch the parade. Mary Ellen wiped a scuff mark off the white donkey stone line of her step before stepping back inside and closing the door.

The arrival of the procession of fair folk meant that feast week was about to begin: A great red traction engine with its smoking stovepipe, smaller wheels to the front and larger ones to the back chugged up the hill. Its elaborate gleaming brass work made it all the more splendid. It would generate enough power for the lights and rides. The traction engine was followed by bright red, yellow, and orange lorries each pulling along 2-3 other vehicles holding the many pieces of the rides, stalls, and tents: Dodgem cars, Round and Round, and peacock blue-colored Dragons.

Everything else on High Street, from the few cars, to the trackless, and Jockey Gee and his cart ground to a halt. One lorry pulled along a trailer filled with 10-12 brownish-gray, long eared donkeys, some of whom stuck their velvety soft muzzles out the bars as they took in the sights and acrid scents of Rawmarsh. The procession took on an even more exotic air as large cob horses with braided manes clop, clop, clopped along, pulling ornate, brightly painted and mirrored vardos— the long, tall caravans that carried the Gypsy—or Traveler— families who followed the fair wherever it went. The Gypsy men were hired as gaffers to set up and break down the various rides and stalls. The Gypsy women, who wore scarves on their heads and long skirts, went from door to door selling laundry pegs and telling fortunes Their children mainly stayed close to and played around the wooden steps of the vardos, staring back at the local children who stared at them.

The fair was the highlight of late summer in Rawmarsh— an event that thrilled Harry and most every other child in the village. For Edna, William, and all the adults in Rawmarsh, the fair was a chance to be wistful—a reminder of childhood before the Great War. Its return after the war was one of the signs that life was more normal and improving.

Harry, Derek, Edgar, and Alan decided to join with other children in running along the procession on High Street, then followed as the procession turned right at Ward's

Greengrocers to head down Stocks Lane, passing the shops and Congregational Church—"The Congo"—toward the Crown Inn and Scales Butchers. It then took a sharp right turn through a gate into the field that, for as long as anyone in Rawmarsh could remember, was transformed into a fairground for fun, feats of skill and strength, and romance.

The fair had its roots in Medieval times, when traveling fairs moved across England from one market town to another. The 1937 fair combined the modern with many of the universally enjoyed Victorian pleasures: Rides like the roundabout with its steam-powered organ in the center playing brass band and marching tunes shared the field with the newer peacock-like dragons that carried 6 to 8 laughing and screaming people per vessel. Then there was the Cake Walk, which challenged those willing to have a go to stay upright on a pivoting, pitching, rotating walkway. Swing boats designed to look like Viking ships were yet another favorite: Fairgoers stepped into oblong vessels of about 5 yards long and 3 yards wide, pivoting back and forth, then back around. A net was placed under the vessels just in case. Best of all, at least to Harry, Derek, Alan, and Edgar, were the dodgem cars—gleaming sedans they could "drive," since none of them had actually ever been in a real car. They were enthusiastic about crashing into each other and anyone else who got in their way.

The boys grew in excitement and impatience as they waited over the next few days for the fair to open. The sight of the donkeys grazing added an air of the seaside rides they knew from the day trips to Cleethorpes and Scarborough sponsored by the working men's clubs. Each donkey had a colorful harness decorated with shiny brass bells and brass nameplates. Harry took a liking to a donkey named Rory that twitched its long ears and stomped its dainty left front hoof. The boys laughed when occasionally one of the donkeys pushed it head forward, bearing its large teeth as if to smile, before braying loudly.

Finally, after what seemed like ages of waiting to the boys, the fair opened. Bright lights on the rides, ropes of lights around the grounds, and the sounds of the confident steam organ playing made Harry feel like a bit of Blackpool had come to Rawmarsh.

Cousins Jack and Ernest Payne came 'round to pick up Harry, the Cooper boys, and Edgar. Nanan had saved up and gave each of the boys a half-shilling apiece. Edna and William gave them each a half-shilling apiece, too. The boys set off in haste, intent to ride the dodgems. When they arrived, they got there just in time to see that another ride, the Waltzer, had a long queue of mostly men and older boys. The ride was anything but a sedate, graceful dance. It had a circular platform that revolved around a track. This rose and fell in an undulating series of hills and dips.

Despite the many rides, Harry's favorite was donkey rides. The sight of them reminded him of the day trip to the seaside at Scarborough he, William, and Edna had taken the previous summer. Each donkey had a bridle with a brass name plate. Harry soon focused in on a favorite named Rory he wanted to ride. Rory seemed to have a sense of humor—an alertness to him—despite what must have been a tedious life of being walked around and around in circles from village to town to village with a steady stream of riders on his back.

"Come on," said Harry, pulling at cousin Jack's sleeve, let's ride the donkeys. Jack smiled and called the other boys. He had no plans to ride the donkeys—deciding they were too small for the likes of a big lad—but he was glad to give Harry time for a go 'round. The older boy cousins and Edgar stood to the side as Harry, Derek, Alan waited their turns. Harry was thrilled when by good luck he ended up being able to ride Rory. He loved being able to view the fairgrounds as he rode, and took in all the sounds—roaring rides, fair folk barkers calling out, "Step right up, ladies and gents...ride the incredible Viking ships..." Harry could see across the fairground as the large swing boats pivoted forward and back higher and higher, with riders holding on tight and squealing as they all but imagined they were sailing over giant waves on the North Sea. It was as close to flying as they could imagine.

As Harry sat on the back of his favorite donkey and took it all in, he couldn't help but feel a wave of joy take hold as he took in the sights, sounds, and scents of the fairground. He was beaming.

When it came time to dismount from Rory after a few times around the circle in the donkey enclosure, Harry lingered a moment to rub Rory's soft muzzle, then, after a wistful look back at his four-legged friend, headed on to the next ride with cousins Jack and Ernest and friends Edgar, Derek, and Alan.

The boys wandered about, catching sight of William and Leonard playing Coconut Shy, where they were aiming to dislodge coconuts that were balanced on posts. If they were successful, they would be able to bring the exotic coconuts home as their prize.

It was one of the rare times when everyone felt like a child, a time when the usual cares faded away for at least a while. No wonder everyone looked forward to it each year.

Far too quickly the bright lights and excitement were gone. The fair was over for another year. Drizzle came down as the travelers began the job of breaking down the rides and preparing to leave Rawmarsh for their next destination. The rides that had been so thrilling to their riders only the night before were now taken apart to load onto the lorries. Harry and the other boys, umbrellas in hand, made their way to watch—and Harry made certain to look for the donkeys being loaded up for transport. He hoped to catch sight of Rory—and soon enough he saw and heard him—braying loudly and stamping his right front foot on the hay strewn beneath his hooves. "See you next time," Harry murmured wistfully.

When all was set, the brightly colored steam tractor engine once again led the way as the animals and rides were driven out of the field and back up Stocks Lane toward High Street. The travelers continued to be a source of fascination—and even a bit more familiar, less "foreign"—

as they were pulled by the horses. Children on the vardos and Harry and the other children watched each other intently—until one dark-eyed girl among the travelers waved shyly. Harry waved back shyly, too.

The colorful procession, somewhat muted in appearance because of the drizzle and gathering storm clouds, headed toward Haugh Road to parts unknown—perhaps to another village somewhere else in the West Riding or beyond. And as the procession moved on and out of sight, life in Rawmarsh became something far less exotic once again.

"Come on then Harry," said Edgar, "They'll be back next year." Harry nodded and followed his friend home. Little did either boy know that the fair that had long been a part of Rawmarsh's life, had just completed its last visit there. Gathering storm clouds in the wider world meant the days of such a spectacle and much-anticipated pastime were coming to an end.

A Fall on High Street

1938

It was the first fine day in two weeks—a day of warm late-spring breezes that took the chill out of the bone and breathed hope into every moment. Edna was glad to be able to hang a load of washing outside for a change. She enjoyed the flap-flap-flapping sound of bedding as the warm air gently lifted and dried the sheets and pillowcases. She was deep in thinking, attaching a shirt to the line and fastening it on with a peg, thinking about a ride later in the day in Joe Wilson's sidecar over the moors to visit sister Elsie's house.

Harry had been glad to take off on his bicycle for a ride in the fine weather, proud to have learned with help from William how to stay balanced while pedaling forward. He loved riding his bicycle and being able to ride it to other streets nearby for adventures on his own or with his friends. Edna liked that his excursions gave her a bit of peace.

And as Edna continued to fasten washing to the line, her peace and quiet was suddenly interrupted by Harry's piercing wail from the front of the house. She dropped her bag of clothes pins into her wicker washing basket and ran inside. Harry stood in the front room sobbing. Blood was trickling down both of his knees and onto his socks.

"Harry, my son, whatever is the matter?" Edna cried out as she rushed forward toward him.

Lost in sobs, he couldn't speak. Instead, rivers of tears streamed down his cheeks.

"Dear lad, what has happened?" Edna asked again as she quickly headed back to the kitchen to fetch a clean rag, water, and iodine to tend to Harry's wounds.

"My bicycle—my bicycle!" Harry cried out, "I fell...off of my bicycle!"

"Oh pet, come sit down and let's take care of your poor knees." Edna led Harry to sit down, then bent down to gently dab them. He continued to sob heavily.

"How did you fall from your bicycle, then?" she asked.

"I-I-I...was riding on High Street...on my way back from...the Cenotaph...near the Earl Grey...There was a lorry coming one way and the trackless was coming toward me, so I rode close to the sidewalk. I guess...I got too close. My pedal hit the curb and...I flew forward over the handlebars and hit the sidewalk." Harry wiped away the stream of tears that kept flowing. Edna pulled out her handkerchief and offered it to him to wipe his nose. Then she saw his scraped elbows, red from the skin hitting the pavement, too.

"Oh son, I am sorry...there, there." said Edna soothingly. Then, just as she expected him to settle down a bit, Harry began to cry even louder than before, overwhelmed with another kind of pain.

"And Mrs. Marriott from church—she saw the whole thing, mummy. She saw me fall! But she didn't help me! She didn't care! She stepped right over me and yelled at me...'*Get out of my way, miner's son!*' She didn't even help me! She acted like she hated me...I didn't do anything wrong! Why was she so mean to me? What's wrong with being a miner's son? Does she hate dada?" Harry sobbed, deeply wounded in spirit.

Edna's face flushed red with anger. "Esther Marriott? You mean the haughty one on the altar guild who always sits up front at church and acts like sweetness and light in front of Canon Scovell?"

"Yes, mummy." Harry sobbed, "I see her all the time when I am at church with Nanan! And she never smiles at us, she always frowns. She's not nice at all!"

Edna was speechless for a moment as the anger flooded her mind at the thought of Esther Marriott not only not helping Harry, but actually going out of her way to be cruel to him.

"You did nothing wrong son—and there's nothing wrong with being the son of a kind, brave, hard-working miner like your dada. If I'm not mistaken, Esther Marriott's home is heated with the coal your dada and men like him mine." Edna felt a stab of pain at the thought of what had just happened to Harry.

He began to sob less, but the pained expression on his face told Edna that Esther Marriott's words stung more than the bad scrapes on his knees. She continued to gently clean up Harry's physical wounds, then brought him a glass of milk and a biscuit, sitting down with him and holding him close.

"You're a fine lad, Harry. What Mrs. Marriott said to you was wrong. Terribly wrong. You know that, don't you son?"

Harry looked into Edna's eyes and smiled weakly, nodding *yes*.

"There, there, Harry. You have a rest for a little while. I need to drop something next door with your Nanan." Edna took the bloodied rag back to the kitchen to be washed, then picked up her flour canister as if Nanan needed some. She went next door.

Nanan immediately saw that Edna was greatly upset. Then, once she heard the whole story, she was as upset as Edna. She knew the likes of Esther Marriott: Like the Pharisees of the New Testament, she made a great display of her religiosity and saw it as her duty to impose rules and rituals of the faith as she saw them on those with little power to challenge her. Nanan had her own experiences with the woman over the years—petty slights and outright meanness. Nanan had always taken it all in stride, turned the other cheek, hurtful as it often was. But this time it had gone well past too far. This unctuous, holier-than-thou woman had deliberately struck out at Harry when he was hurt and vulnerable. Rather than being a help and a balm to the child, she had attacked him for no reason except that she felt entitled to. She was a bully.

Edna and Nanan discussed the matter for a while over tea. They were both upset for Harry. It reminded them of the humiliations they, too, had suffered over the years at the hands of Esther Marriott and too many more like her in Rawmarsh. As the two women sat and contemplated the situation, Nanan made a decision, one which she kept to herself, as she assured Edna that something good would come of this day.

The next morning, Nanan made her way over to St. Mary's in search of Reverend Scovell. She had known him since he first arrived in Rawmarsh before the Great War. She was a busy mother with growing children at the time—and active in the Mother's Union, a group which she still enjoyed being part of even now that her children were grown. Scovell had a true regard for Nanan and so many other poor Rawmarsh mothers who did their level best to make the most of little, feeding, clothing, and raising their children to be kind in unkind surroundings. He had grown to understand many of their struggles, and the struggles of their husbands and sons working at great risk in the mines and steel works. He hadn't always felt that way. Appointed to the living at Rawmarsh by the Lord Chancellor, when he first arrived at St. Mary's he had the airs of the aristocrat that he was and was full of the zeal of the then highly active and vocal Temperance movement. In his very first sermon at St. Mary's he made scathing reference to seeing "a drunk miner" causing a disturbance on a street. His remarks had a chilling effect on how the mining families in his parish viewed him. Things were off to a bad start.

In time he began to understand the terrible pressures they faced each day, the lack of resources, the danger of mining work, why, despite its damaging effects, some men turned to drinking heavily to anesthetize themselves from their daily cares and worries. Before long, Scovell made a point of getting to know the most vulnerable families in his flock and turned his new insights into a compassionate, even affectionate regard for them. Through tending to the families at the birth of their children, their weddings, and at their deaths—which all too often came too young—his caring concern for their welfare led to their reciprocating his regard for them.

Now, on the morning after Harry's encounter with Esther Marriott, Nanan found him in the vestry speaking with two curates. At her arrival, the curates took their cues and made their way out so that Scovell could speak with Nanan.

"Mrs. Bailey, I hope you are well?"

"Reverend Scovell, I am sorry to disturb you, but I've come to speak with you about my grandson Harry."

"Harry? Do come and sit with me." Scovell remembered the rough start he'd had with Harry—questioning his parents about their chosen name for their son—but the relationship had only improved over the years since then.

The kindly clergyman led Nanan to the sanctuary and they sat at one of the pews up front as the stained glass over the altar shone brightly with a tableau of Jesus rising to Heaven.

Nanan described what had happened between Harry and Esther Marriott the day before. He listened intently, noticing the slight tremble of repressed sadness and anger in Nanan's voice, her tired look, and the roughed-up hands of a woman who had never lived a life of ease like Esther Marriott had. Such encounters always softened his heart.

As Nanan finished her report, without hesitation, Reverend Scovell replied gently, "Mrs. Bailey, you can be certain that I will support you and young Harry. I shall ponder what way to go from here, but know that I will address this in a way that causes no further pain for you or your grandson. He's a fine boy. My great disappointment is that the lady in question shows one face to me and clearly another cruel one I don't see to those who have the least power to stop her. I am only too sorry that I have missed this in her before." Nanan felt the warm comfort of being understood.

With that, the tall, patrician Scovell stood up, offered his arm to help Nanan up, and walked with her to the narthex to make her way into the churchyard and home.

"Thank you, sir." Nanan said, feeling as if a great weight had been lifted from her. "Our Harry is a good boy. Thank you for understanding." With that, for the first time that day, a smile spread across and warmed her care-worn face. She knew that Reverend Scovell would be true to his word.

Soon after, Scovell made his way to his home at the vicarage across High Street. It was quiet most of the time these days. The Scovells' four children were mostly grown and away at university or, in the case of son Charles, in Burma working for the Foreign Office. The extensive 18th century rectory had large bay windows and expansive floors, and the lounge held a large tiger skin rug complete with head, glass eyes, and teeth. Charles Scovell had shipped the tiger's pelt to his parents in England after reluctantly shooting it at the pleading of terrified villagers. The rug was what remained of the once powerful animal that, hungry and true to its nature, had killed several people in its quest for food.

Reverend Scovell sat at his desk in his study, the place where he wrote his sermons each week. Light streamed into the room and the occasional traffic sounds made the large window rattle ever so gently. His study offered him a place where he could view and ponder humanity—people passing by on foot, by horse and carriage, by motorcar and lorry, and by the dozens on the trackless. He often gazed out at the street, fascinated and intrigued by all he saw and heard. It was as compelling to him as any film being shown at the Regal just a short distance away. Each week was the same: After watching the world go by for a while for a time, he moved to his desk to write the sermon for Sunday. He pulled out sheets of vellum from his desk, picked up his pen, sat back in his chair for a few minutes, tap-tap-tapped his pen on the desktop a few times, then dipped its nib into the inkwell and began to scratch his thoughts into a sermon.

◆ ◆ ◆

Sunday morning came around. Reverend Scovell and the curates prepared for the services, with the former all the while taking closer note of Esther Marriott's sycophantic chatter in the sacristy as she carried out her altar guild activities, some of which seemed unnecessary and merely gave her an opportunity to linger among the clergy before making her way to the nave and taking a seat in her preferred pew up front close to the altar on the Epistle side of the church. Nanan arrived and took her usual seat further back on the Gospel side. She caught sight of Esther Marriott and felt flush. She studied the hymn numbers posted for the service and opened the hymnal in front of her to divert her attention away from her anger and sense of hurt for Harry—and made a point of greeting Frank Pickering as he carried out his church warden duties.

The service began. Esther Marriott genuflected and crossed herself deeper than the rest of those gathered as Mr.

Allot, the choir director, carried the crucifer and the choir processed toward the altar. After hymns were sung and collects read, Reverend Scovell rose from his chair at the altar and ascended to the pulpit. There, he briefly arranged the pages on which he had written the week's sermon and began.

"Our Lord Jesus's teachings, recorded so long ago, are yet no less relevant now than when he shared them. As Christians, we know the great Parables he shared with those who knew him—and as Christians we look always to model ourselves on his teachings and love. Here in Rawmarsh, these 1,937 years since our Lord's birth, still here in Rawmarsh we, the faithful, look for guidance and recognize the relevance of Jesus's teachings and questions in our daily lives.

"In Luke 10:25-37, we encounter a memorable Parable about loving our neighbors: A lawyer, drawing from Leviticus, asks Jesus 'And who is my neighbor?'

"Jesus replies with the Parable of the Good Samaritan: A traveler is attacked, stripped of his clothing, beaten, and left to die alongside the road. A priest comes upon the traveler and avoids him, then a Levite comes by and also avoids the injured man. Finally, a Samaritan encounters the man. The Jews and the Samaritans despised one another, yet this Samaritan sets that animosity aside, shows mercy, and helps the wounded man. Jesus then tells the lawyer that he, too should 'go and do likewise.'

"Let us remember that when Jesus cast the Samaritan in a positive light, it would have challenged the social norms and expectations of the time. It was, in its essence, provocative. But for Christians, it is not provocative. It is what we are taught as the way to live our lives.

"In Matthew 23:28, we learn more about Jesus's insistence on loving our neighbors, this time addressing the hypocrisy he witnesses among those who make a public show of virtue and goodness, masking their real character and behaviors that do harm to others: 'Even so ye also outwardly appear righteous unto men, but within ye are full of hypocrisy and iniquity.'

"My study at the rectory overlooks High Street with all its comings and goings. Often, as I prepare to write my sermons, I gaze outside at life—people coming and going on foot, by horse and carriage, on bicycle, by trackless, and even occasionally by motorcar. Being able to watch the world go by is comforting most of the time. I see the variety of life—its beauty, frailty. I see the young and old, mothers holding the hands of their children, fathers headed to and from work, a kindly woman or man helping an elderly person go by or step up onto the trackless, the weekly rhythm of tradesmen, school children, miners, managers, well-off, and those who struggle for the very little they have.

"I think about how Rawmarsh is unique, yet how much it reflects the common experience of humanity and even still the conditions of life Jesus knew so well. Like all communities, Rawmarsh has the strong, the weak, the gentle, and the mean. We have our moments of joy and celebration, and moments that cause us pain and grief. We have our moments where who we say we are and how we actually are can either be in harmony—or have a jarring effect on those around us.

"And as I think of the view from the rectory to the stage that is High Street, I cannot help but grieve at a recent event there: A young boy of this parish, a child under our very wings, fell off of his bicycle not far from where we sit today. He was injured in body and spirit. His knees bled and his elbows were red and stinging, their skin scraped off from hitting the hard surface. Dazed, in pain, he lay stunned on the pavement—with his bicycle twisted and bent beside him. Blood had begun to trickle from his knees. A woman approached. Rather than helping the child, she injured him further with angry, hurtful words, treating him with scorn, insulting him and diminishing his loving father, a man born into and raised in this parish. Rather than help the injured child, she stepped right over the child, hissing 'Get out of my way, miner's son!' as she continued on her way.

"When I heard of this incident, it pained me greatly—and when I learned that the woman who stepped over the child is one who has always shown me an entirely different affect, who takes an active role in our parish life, it pains me. I think back to the Good Samaritan of the Book of Luke and I think about what Jesus teaches us about hypocrisy in Matthew.

"I take notice of this incident because it is instructive to all of us. Christian life is not about the appearance of virtue, but about loving our neighbors as ourselves. Matthew 25:40-45 underscores this: 'Verily I say unto you, Inasmuch as ye have done it unto one of the least of these my brethren, ye have done it unto me' and thinking of wilfully passing by an injured child on the street we share. In the name of the Father, the Son, and the Holy Ghost. Amen."

With that, Mr. Scovell briefly surveyed the congregation without a hint as to whom he had directed his sermon.

Esther Marriott sat all but immobile in her pew staring straight ahead, her pale face even more so than usual. She dared not look at Scovell, knowing that his sermon was directed at her.

Nanan gently dabbed her eyes of tears welling in them, her face sanguine, reflecting the optimism and gratitude she felt that Scovell had taken Harry's experience to heart.

Everyone else drew their own conclusions on who the sermon had been intended for. Many who had experienced Esther Marriott's meanness each arrived at the same conclusion that it was her.

Harry never again experienced the bullying behavior from her that he had. And Reverend Scovell kept a watchful eye not only on Esther Marriott from that time forward, but a caring eye for Harry as the young boy grew up in front of him.

A Terrifying Loss

1938

Queen Victoria was in the middle years of her 54-year reign when Moxon's Yard was built. In the ensuing decades the families who called its dwellings home were intimately familiar with tragedy interspersed with carrying on their daily lives. Under the very roofs where the Baileys, Coopers, Charlesworths, Jacques, and other families lived now there had, in previous generations, been heartbreaking deaths of infants and children in the families who lived there before them. Between 1897 and 1899 alone, out of the twelve households on the row, two babies died—one at just fourteen days and the other at seven months of age.

What saved the neighbors who lived there most of the time was their clear understanding that what kept them afloat was sticking together day-in-and day-out and, in the best moments, kindhearted humor and mutual generosity with what little they had. Their survival—physical and emotional—depended on it.

But, now, in 1938, a new age of modern technology became more visible, perhaps best embodied by the sleek aeroplanes that occasionally flew high above on a rare clear day. Elegant, powerful motorcars—most distinctively the Earl Fitzwilliam's yellow-liveried Rolls Royces—purred gently on the roads between Wentworth and Rawmarsh to and from Rotherham and well beyond. Wireless broadcasts conveyed richly toned voices and music through invisible signals that linked Rawmarsh to Sheffield, Sheffield to London, king to subject, country to king, and frequently Britain to its vast and far-flung empire.

Rawmarsh's especially high infant and maternal mortality rate—which rose only a few years earlier with the economic devastation of the depression—dropped noticeably by 1937 when industry picked up and the mines were operating more steadily. With more money in their pockets, families were beginning to eat better and make some economic headway.

Fortunately, too, the children living on Moxon's Yard—Derek, Alan, Edgar, and Harry—were a largely healthy, energetic bunch who rarely missed a day of school. Doctor O'Connell and other doctors in the village were increasingly able to help the patients on their panels get care in ways that were simply not possible in previous generations.

But despite the exciting technological, social, and scientific advances, the inability to pay for medical care still meant that poor families too often went without care when they needed it most. The families still relied on home remedies or waited until things went too far before seeking help. There was a National Health Insurance scheme started under Chancellor David Lloyd George in 1911—but it was a patchwork system: Extremely limited coverage of access to hospital and no dependent care coverage were troubling aspects of the system that evolved from the plan. Workers— typically male—and their employers contributed to it in almost equal parts. The contribution rate was not graduated based on income level. It only covered hospitalization for tuberculosis. It did not provide hospital coverage for any other illness. Both hospitalization costs and having a medical attendant at birth could be financially crippling for poor families. Since the scheme did not cover dependents, families paid in what little they could—6 pence a week whenever possible—to their doctor's office for care in case something serious happened. Mr. Lister from Dr. O'Connell's office came by Moxon's Yard every Monday to collect the 6-weekly fee. Some weeks the families could not pay in.

The Coopers, the Baileys, the Makins, and all poor working families across Britain were at a distinct disadvantage: They tended to hold off on seeking help with the hope that a home remedy, and a wait-and-see would lead to recovery. This too frequently led to catastrophic results. Late diagnosis could mean prolonged suffering or death. There were still illnesses that were dangerous to everyone, especially children, no matter what station in life: Tuberculosis, Meningitis, Scarlet Fever, Polio, and ear infections still lurked—and treatment options, while progressing, remained limited.

And so, when Edgar Makin, who had suffered from ear infection before, showed signs of ear infection again, Mary Ellen first did what all poor families did when they couldn't afford a trip to the doctor: She decided to take a wait and see approach. He had recovered before. She tried home remedies like castor oil and cotton wool in his ears and other "cures" from the chemist. But this time was different. His pain and symptoms grew worse each day. Edgar, always an energetic and cheerful soul, ever a "brave lad," was ill for a long time and cried from the pain, which worsened each night as he lay in his bed downstairs in the front room.

Harry heard the cries through the wall between the families' houses at night. The sound of his friend in such pain frightened him. He curled up under his blankets and wept, blocking his ears hoping to block out the terrible sound of his friend's anguish. He felt helpless as Edgar's wails pierced through the walls in the darkness. He wanted to go and comfort Edgar, but he was also afraid of what he would see if the Coopers let him in. Edna and William heard the wrenching cries, too, of course. There was no way they wouldn't. They were all alarmed for Edgar. Several nights in a row, as Edgar cried next door, Edna lit a candle, got up, and came into Harry's room, finding him weeping quietly under his covers. She sat down with him, gathered him in her arms, and gently rocked him. Tears dropped from her eyes onto his blanket.

No combination of hope, time, and home remedy was going to cure Edgar. His balance was off. Sweat dripped off of him. Daylight was overbearing for him, so he sat in darkness. The pain worsened at night after night. Discharge started to pour from his ear. He began vomiting.

Mary Ellen sent word to Doctor O'Connell's Westfield Road surgery for him to come to the house. Edgar's dad had no choice but to continue on, like William, working as normal at the pit. Mary Ellen sent Derek and Alan off to school along with Harry. None of the three boys wanted to leave Moxon's Yard. As soon as they were gone, Edna came next door to be with Mary Ellen and Edgar.

Mary Ellen's face was pale with fear. Edgar had developed palsy on one side of his face. He was clearly racked with fever. He was delirious, drifting in and out of consciousness. Edna did her best to hide her shock at the sight of the poor lad. She had never seen a child suffer so much.

Dr. O'Connell arrived shortly after, his well-worn brown leather medical bag in hand. He was a kindly man, much respected by Rawmarsh families, poor and better off alike, a reputation earned over decades of caring for families there, for his compassion and for listening with care. He was a distinctive sight, one who enjoyed smoking cigars when he was not tending to patients directly.

When he stepped into the house he moved straight to Edgar, who was lying in the front room, shaking on the settee. He looked into and around Edgar's right ear and saw the distinct redness, swelling, and discharge of advanced Mastoiditis. This meant a middle ear infection had spread to the part of the bumpy temporal bone behind the ear containing open, air-containing pockets. Given what he was seeing along with Edgar's other symptoms, it was highly probable that his ear infection had spread to his brain, the stage at which ear infection becomes deadly. Possible surgery in hospital was the only chance of survival for him. And it was a slim one.

What Dr. O'Connell saw told him all he needed to know. "There my lad," he spoke gently to Edgar. "You rest easy while I have a quick word with your sister outside." Dr. O'Connell and Mary Ellen gently lowered Edgar down and replaced the brown-stained pillow under his head as he sunk from barely conscious into unconsciousness again.

The doctor gently signaled to Mary Ellen and Edna to step outside. Nanan and some of the other neighbors had gathered outside to wait for news. They saw the doctor's expressions change in a flash from serious and alert to a deeply sad and back again as he quickly re-composed himself. He turned to Mary Ellen and put a comforting hand on her arm. Her face was mottled from crying. She had barely slept for days.

Shielding her from lookers on, he spoke gently to Mary Ellen, "Mrs. Cooper, this is a serious case of infection. Your young brother is in real danger. I know you understand that. I only wish that I had seen the poor lad much sooner. We don't have much chance to stop this. We must get him to hospital if there's to be any chance at all. We'll need to ring for an ambulance from the police station. You must reach your father. Who can go find him at the pit?" He paused, then added, "There's little time."

Mary Ellen nodded her understanding, then bowed her head. She felt an overwhelming mix of helplessness and anger at herself for not acting sooner. Her despair burned at her spirit. Her fear for her younger brother was overwhelming. He was, after all, still a child. She was lost in painful rumination, but not for long: She could hear Edgar, briefly returned to consciousness, shouting in delirium inside. His ears stung and his head throbbed with overwhelming pain.

"Mary Ellen," said Edna thinking for her friend, "I'll run up t' the police and ask them to call an ambulance and see if they can speed word to your dad at the pit." Mary Ellen nodded. Edna wasted no time in dashing home, collecting her purse, then heading to the police station, where she explained the situation to the officer on duty there. Seeing Edna's anguish and realizing the situation, he wasted no time in contacting an ambulance and getting the word out to Aldwarke Main to call for Edgar's dad so that he could meet his daughter and son at the hospital on Moorgate in Rotherham. It would take some time for the colliery to get word to Edgar's dad underground, and an agonizing time for him to travel underground to the surface to get to the hospital to his son.

When Derek, Alan, and Harry returned from school for lunch they arrived at the sight of St. John's Ambulance parked in front of the Cooper's house at Number 19. Edna had returned from the police station, had made their lunch, and had been waiting for them. With the windows open to keep the house cool, they expected to hear Edgar crying, but his cries had lessened, not because he was in less pain, but because, once again, he was barely conscious. Mary Ellen came to the door briefly. Her expression of fear and devastation spoke volumes. Derek and Alan ran up to hug her, then stepped back from the door, their eyes riveted to it, waiting for Edgar to be brought out. Harry, Edna, and Nana stood by them.

A small crowd of neighbors, shopkeepers, and curious passers-by assembled. The matinee cinemagoers at the Regal lined up for tickets alongside Moxon's Yard watched as the real-life drama unfolded before them.

The ambulance crew soon emerged carrying a thin, pale Edgar out of the house on a stretcher. They gently lifted him up and settled him in the back of the ambulance. Then one of the attendants helped Mary Ellen up and into the ambulance, where she sat down next to Edgar and took her little brother's hand. Edna passed up Mary Ellen's coat and a bag with Edgar's belongings in it. The attendants inside then gently pulled the door shut. The boys lost sight of their friend.

The driver revved the engine, released the clutch, then carefully made a three-point turn to reverse the ambulance over the sandstone and dirt yard to head back onto High Street.

The boys had walked alongside it to the top of Moxon's Yard. The ambulance turned left onto High Street, then proceeded down the hill. The boys watched as it picked up speed down Rawmarsh Hill toward Rotherham. Pedestrians, carts, and the few cars stopped, pulled over to the side to make way for it and the trackless headed in the same direction stayed in place 'til it had passed.

Edna, shaken with deep sadness herself, also watched down the hill as the ambulance sped away. Then, after they all lingered staring down the hill for a few minutes, watching life around them move back to normal, she gathered the boys around her, then led them toward the Bailey household. There would be no returning to school that afternoon. The boys needed to be together. Nanan met them at the house and helped Edna feed the boys lunch, which they picked at slowly. Sorrow and fear overcame hunger. No one spoke a word.

Edgar Makin died two days later in hospital. His father and sister were by his side at the end. Edgar's mother was not in the picture. She had left the family years before. Because his ear infection had spread to his brain and poisoned his blood there was no medicine, no cure to save him. He was thirteen years old.

Harry was only eight when Edgar died. It devastated and frightened him. He began to have nightmare in which Edgar appeared weeping, making Harry fearful of falling asleep. All this was compounded by gnawing worry that he, too, could die the same way. He had never experienced the death of someone he knew, never mind a lively, kind friend. Edgar had been the big brother, a protector to all the younger boys on the yard. Even though he was uncle to Derek and Alan, he was much more a mate to them because he was closer in age to them than his sister. After another boy had thrown Harry into the swimming baths before he knew how to swim, causing him to thrash in terror in the water, it was Edgar who had patiently coaxed him back into the water over several visits there. Edgar's sense of humor, warmth, and adventure made every day special in some way. *How could someone so full of life suffer and then be gone?* Harry wondered about this over and over in the months after Edgar was gone. He felt as if he were drowning in grief.

Everyone on the yard was scarred by Edgar's death in some way.

Ever so slowly, time healed the painful wound of the loss. Edgar's father moved away—away from the pain of Edgar's death that made it too hard to stay in the very place where he had suffered so much. Like Mary Ellen, he agonized over not taking Edgar to the doctor sooner. Everyone else had to find a way to move forward beyond this profound sadness and the void left by Edgar's passing.

In time, while the sadness never truly went away, its pain eased. Finally, there came a time when the families could speak about Edgar and laugh at the many wonderful ways he had touched their lives. Harry vowed to never forget his friend—and he never did.

Christmas and the New Year's Eve with the Family

1938

Edna's kitchen was a hive of activity and dishes piled high in the sink awaiting a wash up as she prepared for the early evening arrival of the extended Dyson, Payne, and Bailey families. Harry looked forward to a house full of his cousins— including Elsie, Audrey, Irene, Dorothy, Ernest, Jack, and Dennis, who was a keen and talented footballer. Harry hoped his older cousin might show off some of his fancy footwork with a ball. But first, before any play, Edna put Harry to work rolling up newspaper tightly, then knotting the bundles and placing them in a basket by the fire to use for kindling to build a large fire to warm up the front room when everyone arrived. It was New Year's Eve, a time when much of the extended family all gathered for a sing-along and the First Footing—the time after midnight of the new year when the family welcomed a dark-haired, handsome young man as the first to step foot into the house, bringing good luck and gifts to the family. Everyone hoped the new year 1939 would be a happy, prosperous, healthy, and peaceful one.

"William, be a love and take these and place them on the sideboard in the front room," Edna said as she handed him a plate full of the mince tarts. "Tah then."

William carried the plates of cheese, ham, and biscuits to the sideboard by the fireplace in the front room, then took several of the newspaper bundles Harry had rolled and set them in the fire, along with a generous heaping of coal to build an especially bright fire.

One element of the evening plans added tension to the occasion, as it did with every family occasion. John Edward would arrive in state. Harry truly dreaded his grandfather's visits because it was inevitable that the patriarch would have something critical to say about each of them.

Feeling anxious about this, Harry said, "Mum, why must grandfather come to our house? He never has anything nice to say to us—and he always wants me to play *Salut d'Amour* on the piano, then hovers over me and makes me nervous so I make mistakes. Last time he hit my knuckles when I hit a wrong note. Irene and Dorothy feel the same way as I do. They both play so well—but not when he's around. We're all thumbs. Why is he always so mean?"

Though he agreed, William responded, "That's no way to speak about your grandfather, Harry."

"But dada, he makes all of us children so uncomfortable. He never has a kind word!" protested Harry.

"What do you think I should do?" chimed in Edna, already tense and now upset as Harry's comments brought out into the open the feeling of dread that each of them felt when her father was present.

"I don't know," said Harry, "I just want us to have fun tonight and grandfather seems to enjoy making sure we don't."

Edna became pensive and William looked pained. As soon as he saw that his comments upset them, Harry wished he had kept his thoughts to himself. After a bit of silence, Edna said, "You're right, son. Your grandad is difficult. He has been that way for as long as I can remember. I understand that it's hard when he visits. It's hard on me, your dad, your aunties and uncles. We can either let that ruin our fun or we can accept that he's not going to change and live our lives the best way we can and remember everyone around us who cares for us. I'm not going to make excuses for him, but under all of it he'd be daft if he didn't see how wonderful you and your cousins are. Don't pay him any mind."

Harry thought about this for a while and realized that, although he found time with John Edward to be difficult, Edna was onto something with her advice to not let her father have that much power over everyone.

Harry went quiet as he re-focused on the fun family times and New Year's Eve festivities to come.

When at last everyone gathered for the evening, it wasn't long after coats were off and hung that the singing began. Edna and her sisters chimed together and giggled their way through many of their favorite songs, including ones that were popular when they were teens during the Great War:

"Daisy, Daisy, give me your answer true. I'm half-crazy all for the likes of you. It won't be a stylish marriage. I can't afford a carriage. But you'll look sweet upon the seat of a bicycle built for two."

Everyone clapped and laughed, except John Edward, who sat stiffly in the corner, not one to join in the fun. Still, Harry did notice him tapping his foot to the beat of the music at one point as everyone else sang.

When Midnight was finally close at hand, the anticipation grew: Out with the old year and in with the new. William reminded the children that with a bit of luck the First Footer would soon be there—usually a handsome young man with dark hair came knocking on the door and was the first person to enter the house on New Year's Day to bring good fortune for the year to come.

Harry was growing weary as midnight passed, but he was determined not to miss the first footer and the promise of good fortune. He was excited that the first footer would bring coins for the children, and very likely other treats and whisky for the grownups.

Soon after the clock struck midnight and the start of 1939, there was a loud knock on the outside door. Cheered on by the family, William went to open it—and in stepped Tommy Jacques. Harry was delighted to see his neighbor and local cricket hero in the role of First Footer. He was even more pleased when Tommy began to distribute coins to all the children. Last but not least, Tommy proffered a bottle of whisky to the adults—and each raised a glass to toast Tommy and the New Year. Tommy stayed for a bit to enjoy a mince tart and warm himself by the fire before continuing to more homes. Just before he left, he turned to Harry and said, "Just a minute young Harry, I think there's something outside the door for you." Harry eagerly moved toward Tommy as he opened the door and reached to something learning against the brick of the outside wall. "What is this I have here?" said Tommy, with a twinkle in his eye. Harry moved even closer to Tommy and the front door. "Why gracious me!" continued Tommy, "It's a cricket bat! And it's for you!"

Harry jumped up and down with excitement as Tommy Jacques passed the bat to him, then he held it close and took pride in showing it to everyone. The bat had been lying about the Rawmarsh Cricket Ground unclaimed for all to the previous season. Tommy, knowing that Harry didn't have a bat, decided at the end of the season to bring it home for him. He let William in on the surprise ahead of time and they agreed that the First Footing would be a wonderful time to surprise Harry with it.

"Thank you, Tommy!" Harry cried out with excitement. "Thank you, Thank you!" He spun around on his heel in excitement. Even Grandad Dyson was hard pressed not to smile at least a little.

1939 was off to a grand start—and Harry could barely wait for spring so he could get together with his friends to play outside with his new bat.

Setback and a Jump Ahead

1939

At seven years old, Harry was so far ahead of his form academically that the teachers at Dale Road School realized that he was ready for and needed a greater challenge. After some discussion among the headmaster and teachers and a meeting with Edna, Harry was moved up to be with students two years older than he was, leaving the friends his age to study with the older children.

Harry rose to and mostly enjoyed the challenge of the more advanced work. His teachers were encouraging, and he did well in the classroom. He loved to read. *The Jungle Book* and *The Wind in the Willows* became his favorite books. He looked forward to his weekly visits to the Carnegie where, since Miss Allot had recommended it to Edna, he had read the *Illustrated London News* every week, studying the photographs for clues to life in the wider world.

Being two years younger than his classmates was also difficult. The older children were developmentally ahead of him—and he was smaller than they were. In the first weeks, a few students bullied him, pushing his books off his desk when the teachers' backs were turned, tripping him as he walked past them. He did his best to take it in stride but that wasn't always easy, and he felt anxious. Other students became protective of him, treating him like a mascot of sorts, a likeable, smart younger friend. Having older cousins meant that Harry could hold his own if he needed to. Cousins Jack and Ernest, when they learned that some boys had given Harry trouble, rounded on them outside of school, exerting their influence to protect their young cousin. Harry was glad to have their support.

The rougher, back-handed treatment stopped, and Harry was able to delve into his studies and making older friends. Most of the students liked Harry and got used to having a younger boy among them. They recognized his deep intelligence and likeable nature. He became one of them in time, even making friends with two of the older boys who had been the first to make him feel unwelcome.

These years at Dale Road were critical ones. Most students would leave school at 14 to go to work, finishing school at the Rawmarsh New Council School on Haugh Road. From there they would likely go down the pit or, perhaps, enter a trade, work in a shop, or do factory work. Others, with the right encouragement at home, academic abilities, and money to pay for it from families or a limited number of scholarships would try to get a much-coveted grammar school place. The odds of getting in were small, but in the past few years a few Rawmarsh students had been successful. Horace Bailey was among them. He was accepted on academic scholarship to Mexborough School—but then had to wait for an actual place to open up. Horace couldn't help but notice that students his age who had money and got into Mexborough seemed to be offered a place earlier than he was.

The possibility of grammar school seemed a long way off to Harry at nine. Once Horace started sharing stories about what it offered, Harry, too, dreamt of going to Mexborough when he was bigger.

To get into grammar school he'd need to do well on a national exam, administered to students at age 11. Success or

171

failure on the exam set a child's educational path for life. A pass meant the chance to continue to grammar school until 18. A fail meant leaving school at 14, still a child, to enter an adult world of dead end, hard manual labor.

Harry was all nerves in the days leading up to the exam, which he was taking two years younger than his classmates. He could barely eat or sleep. Then, the day before the exam, he awoke with a fever, his body aching all over. Edna was desperate for him to be well and covered him with cool towels to try to bring his temperature down. If he didn't take the exam the next day his chances were all but over for a chance to prepare for grammar school.

The following morning Harry was doing little better, but he was able to sit up more than he had the day before. Edna decided he had to go to school and do his best on the exam. She walked with him to make sure he got there.

Once at school, everything was all seriousness as the teachers and students got down to work. Harry sat in his seat, wracked with anxiety, aching and sweating, and his head throbbing. He took the exam but struggled mightily to finish it before returning home and straight back to bed.

When the results came, they were a disaster for Harry: He had failed the exam. His dream of following Horace to Mexborough School came crashing down.

William and Edna pleaded with the school for him to have the chance to take it again the following year, but they were told that it wasn't possible.

The extended family got involved, with Edna's brother Harold urging her and William to petition the education board. They dressed in their Sunday best for the meeting and were clearly nervous addressing the well-heeled educators while pleading Harry's case.

The response was far from encouraging: "Mr. and Mrs. Bailey, anyone can say their child needs another chance, but that chance happened when your son took the exam. He was either not prepared or not suitable grammar school material. I am sorry to say that we can't bend on that."

"But he is nine years old!" pleaded Edna, finding courage within herself she wasn't sure until that moment that she had. She continued, "He's two years younger than all the other students taking the exam with him—and he was ill. Please, please give him another chance. This will harm his chances, harm him for the rest of his life if he can't take the exam again."

At last a concession: "We'll consider the age difference and get back to you."

Two weeks later a letter arrived in the mail for Edna and William. The education authorities had agreed that Harry could take the exam again—in two years' time when he was eleven. He was to return to study with children his own age until then.

It was in some ways a big loss for Harry—he was all but repeating what he had already studied and biding his time until he could take the exam again in two years—but it was the break he needed to stay on course for possibly being able to pass and earn a place in a grammar school. Until then, Edna committed herself to doing all she could to encourage Harry and connect him to people who would lift his spirits and appreciate his intelligence. And Harry still had Horace to mentor and encourage him.

Life Around the Cinemas

Summer 1939

Edna couldn't help but smile as she overheard Harry, Derek, and Alan planning their next chance to see the films and film stars they liked best: *Flash Gordan*, Larry, Curly, and Moe of *The Three Stooges*, or Gene Autry, the Singing Cowboy. Harry still had a special place in his heart for Shirley Temple. Rawmarsh's cinemas were a welcome change from the drab grayness of everyday life, often for very little in exchange. Stepping inside offered an exciting world where, increasingly, it was a pleasure to see films in bold Kinemacolor or Technicolor.

"Mum," said Harry, quickly opening the front door from outside to find Edna sitting by the fire darning a pair of his socks one Saturday morning, "Do you have an empty jam jar I can take to Robbie's Cinema? I can get into penny rush for either a jam jar or a penny!"

"Yes, Harry, Nanan gave me a jam jar for you just yesterday. Pop back into the kitchen. It's on the shelf next t' the mangler," replied Edna.

"Oh, tah, mum!" Harry was all too glad to collect the jar and head off with his friends to the Princess Cinema—better known as Robbie's Cinema. It was housed in a former Methodist chapel on High Street. During penny rush, children could gain entrance to Robbie's in exchange for a jam jar— and get an orange, too.

The boys liked to joke that the old velvet curtains that hung on both side of the screen at Robbie's were so full of dust that if they fell the dust would kill everyone. Its proprietor, Robbie, cut a colourful figure in Rawmarsh as he strode along the main thoroughfares. He was a local celebrity in his own way and had the flair of a showman. He held a long cigar in his mouth and sported a large American-style "ten-gallon" cowboy hat on his head—the very embodiment of a cowboy from the American West.

His wife, "Mean Mrs. Robbie," did not enjoy the same level of admiration from Rawmarsh children: She kept order within the cinema by carrying a big stick she used to keep the boisterous children in line. Focused on maximizing profit, she did not waste a space in any row, packing the children in tightly on long benches. Often a child fell off the cram-packed bench at the furthest end from her and had to run down the side aisle, back to the center aisle, and try to squeeze back into their row again without coming in contact with her scowl and her stick.

At home on Moxon's Yard after their penny rush adventures, the boys also loved playing on top of, around, and beside the Regal. One summer morning Derek climbed up the drainpipe onto the Regal roof. Edna was just coming outside to polish and line her front step when she looked up and caught sight of him as he waved down and smiled at her. "Oh my God!" she burst out as she dropped her bucket of water and donkey stone, then rushed next door, to alert Mary Ellen Cooper. A moment later, Derek's mother was out the door. "Derek!" she called out sternly, "You come down right now!" Derek wasted no time in shimmying his way back down the drainpipe to face his mother's wrath.

Soon after, on a light summer evening, the adults' peace was shattered by the boys' antics at the Regal.

"Mr. Bailey, Mr. Bailey!" yelled Derek.

"Dad, Dad!" shouted Harry.

First the Cooper brothers, then Harry sped urgently from the field behind the Regal toward William, who had only minutes before returned from weeding at the allotment and set a stool up outside the house on the warm summer's evening to enjoy the light and warmth.

Their friend, Alfie Turton, was conspicuously absent from the pack of boys.

"What is it lads?" William asked as he sprung to his feet at the urgency in the boys' voices.

Each boy answered in quick succession:

"Alfie—he's hurt!" shouted Derek.

"Alfie, it's Alfie!" shouted Alan Cooper.

"Alfie—he was jumping off the coal shed at the back of the Regal. But he fell through the roof!" added Harry.

"Steady on, lads, let's go!" said William as he rose quickly from where he sat.

Doors opened and heads popped out up and down Moxon's Yard as the neighbors came out to see what the noise was all about.

Following the boys' lead, William quickly followed them back toward the Regal's coal shed. Taking a peek inside, he saw a coal-dust smeared, teary Alfie Turton lying awkwardly on top of the shed's pile of coal. Sunshine poured through the jagged new hole in the asphalt roof.

"My arm, Mr. Bailey—I can't move my arm! It's broke. My arm!" wailed Alfie.

William gently felt Alfie's arm for signs of a break. He'd seen enough men break limbs down the pit to know to at least start there.

"Alfie, I don't feel any breaks, but come on lad, let me take you to our house and have a proper look." He scooped him up into his arms and gently carried him toward number 21 with all the other boys following closely behind.

Patrons lining up for tickets to the Regal looked on in curiosity at all the excitement.

Edna met them at the door as William brought Alfie into the Baileys' front room and gently placed him in his own armchair next to the hearth.

Nanan, who had heard all the commotion, came over from next door to see what the noise was all about.

"Ow! Ow! I've broke my arm!" Alfie wailed repeatedly. "I've broke my arm!"

"Now then, Alfie." said William soothingly, getting Alfie to stay still. He began to feel up and down Alan's arm again.

"I've broke my arm, it's broken!!" Alfie cried out all over again.

Then Alfie fell silent for a bit, as William gently pressed up and down his arms. Everything felt fine, plus in all the wailing he saw that Alfie had moved the arm with no trouble. "I've broke my arm! I've broke my arm! I'll never be able to play for Yorkshire County Cricket Club now!" Alfie added with an added dramatic flourish, referring to his now-apparently-dashed dreams of a career as a bowler for the county's hallowed team.

William sat up straight and delivered his prognosis to Alfie, "You've not broken your arm, Alfie. You've broken the bloody Regal roof!"

With that Alfie fell silent. The other boys looked at him, then each other, and burst into laughter as they thought back to the scene of Alfie standing on the coal shed roof, preparing to take a dramatic leap to the grassy mound below it to escape from imagined pirates, then disappearing from sight as he fell through the roof into a heap of coal in the shed.

Alfie had a briefly defiant look on his face, then started to laugh, too, while still wiping away tears from his eyes and cheeks. In his unexpected fall he had, in fact, made a big hole in the Regal's coal shed roof. There was no denying it.

Alfie smiled sheepishly at everyone. "Ta, then, Mr. Bailey." William gave Alfie a gentle rub on his arm, helped him up, then brushed some coal dust off of Alfie's backside. Edna brought him a wet cloth so he could wipe his face clean. In a pack the boys headed back out the door toward the field they had just left, not wanting to waste another minute on such a fine day.

William chuckled as he returned to his seat outside. Frank Pickering, who had heard Alfie's wailing from up the top of Moxon's Yard, came down the slope to join William, offering him a packet of Fred Whitlam's fish & chips. Nanan greeted Frank, smiled with relief that Alfie was all right, then stepped back into her house.

Before long the energetic sounds of boys at play on a fine summer's evening filled the air—but they stayed clear of the Regal's coal shed with its newly open roof.

Horace Bailey

1939

One of the greatest gifts in life is having a rich friendship built on mutual caring, affirmation, outlook, and interests. Horace Bailey became that friend and positive influence for Harry. Five years older, he was someone Harry could look up to—and whose temperament was protective of his younger Bailey friend.

Both boys came from mining families. Horace was born in 1925 to Thomas and Evelyn Bailey on Ashwood Road in Parkgate, just before the young family move to Swinton, where they rented a house on Duke Street. Horace's sister Margaret was born there. Thomas became seriously ill, steadily decreasing his ability to work, 'though he desperately tried to work. His meagre wages dropped, then dried up altogether. Then Thomas died. Horace was four years old when he peered at his father's immobile features in the open pinewood casket that filled the family's front room as they prepared to bury him. Horace had lost his protector, the father who loved and played with him before becoming ill. The death had an immediate and catastrophic effect on the devastated young family. Evelyn could no longer afford to live in the house they rented in Swinton. And 'though her husband had several brothers, they, too, were struggling miners with families and too many mouths to feed under their rooves. They couldn't take on the feeding, clothing, and housing of their brother's widow, their nephew and niece, too. A grieving Evelyn had no choice financially but to leave behind the home she had made with Thomas and move back to home with Horace and Margaret to live with their grandfather Dunhill. Horace's grandfather had been a colliery stonemason as a younger man. He had re-built the tower of St. Mary's when it became unstable in the decades earlier. Sadly, he died soon after Evelyn, Horace, and Margaret moved in to live with him. They were once again in a desperate situation. She found accommodation in Parkgate on Ashwood Road in Rawmarsh, crowding into a rented, deteriorating two-up, two down dwelling.

Evelyn looked for whatever work she could find while raising two young children: sewing, mending, doing laundry for others, working herself to exhaustion day after. She received miserly public assistance in the form of 6/8d a week per child at a time when a tin of beans cost 7d and a pint of milk 1d—wholly inadequate for clothing and providing a healthy, adequate, varied diet for two growing children.

One thing became clear quickly to any caring adult who encountered Horace as he grew up: He was exceptionally intelligent and a quick learner. Little did they know something else also fuelled the thin, talented, intense boy dressed in clothing that was beyond well worn. In response to the trauma of watching his father waste away and die, Horace had decided that he would become a doctor—a seemingly outlandish, impractical aspiration for a boy of his poor circumstances and place in society. But Horace was bound and determined.

Canon Scovell was among those who cared. He saw the innate intelligence Horace possessed. Concerned for Horace's wellbeing, he found ways to ensure that he had responsibilities within parish life to expand his horizons. He sent him home with food and clothes.

Horace had real musical talents—as a chorister and in teaching himself and playing the harmonium and the organ.

Before long he was also to be found helping the St. Mary's organist with cleaning the instrument's pipes, valves, and maintaining its overall functioning.

As Harry and Horace grew up, Canon Scovell saw a real opportunity: Both Bailey boys were inordinately gifted, both came from struggling families, and both would benefit from someone else who appreciated those gifts. The clergyman made sure that each had the other for support. Scovell shared his view with his curates on staff—and spoke with the choir director, Mr. Allott, about the younger and older boy. It didn't take much formal encouragement for Horace to help Harry. The two naturally connected well. Horace was supportive as Harry, who had joined the choir and had a fine boy soprano voice, navigated his new role in the various services they both sang in. Horace committed himself to be a mentor to his younger friend. With his guidance, Harry grew in confidence, whether singing on Sunday morning, 6:00 p.m. Evensong, or at a Saturday wedding, or at a funeral. Both boys flourished through the new friendship. Each recognized that they were better together. Horace enjoyed Harry's quick intelligence and gentle spirit. Harry looked up to Horace as a kind, wise, and interesting friend, the brother he had often wished for. Before long, it was hard to tell that the two Bailey boys *weren't* brothers. They were just what each other needed in their lives—accomplices of a positive sort, both eager to make something more of their lives than they could see around them. Something inside both of them wanted to take flight.

"Tha's Not Going Down the Mine, Young Dek"

1939

Summer afternoons and evenings on Moxon's Yard brought most everyone outside. Even Mrs. Hopkinson—"Mother Hop" to the boys—came out, if mainly to frighten off the children when they came too close to her doorstep. To make ends meet, she had a lodger in her house—one with a wooden leg, which he kept by the front door for when he was going out. Mother Hop would come out swinging the wooden leg to chase the boys away from playing near her door, shouting, "Scram, you lot!" Harry, Derek, Alan, and their friends were in parts fearful of the leg and at other times, if far enough from her, laughed ever so hard when they saw her come at them with the ungainly contraption.

Most summer evenings after the Baileys, Coopers, Pickerings, and other neighbors and friends gathered with stools at the top of the yard to watch the world go by on High Street. Mr. and Mrs. Parkin at No. 9 sat outside with everyone, but Mr. Parkin was blind because of a pit accident so he depended on a friendly arm to get there and conversation in place of people watching.

Sometimes the air was filled with the sweet-savory scent of Mrs. Head's cooking closer to the top of the yard and High Street. She ran a business out of the front room of her house at No. 3 selling her piccalilli, sweets, herbals, and other remedies.

When the weather was fine enough, the families on Moxon's Yard would go sit on the bench at the top of the yard facing High Street and Pearson's Fruit Shop across the way. Edna and Mary Ellen Cooper brought up jugs of tea while the menfolk headed across High Street to Freddy Whitlam's Fish Shop for fish and chips for the grown-ups and three pennyworth—or threppence—of fish bits for the boys. If it was Thursday, Freddy Whitlam had fresh rabbit for sale, so Edna made rabbit stew, which Harry loved.

Most exciting of all for the boys was when Tommy Jacques, the local Rawmarsh cricket hero, came out to coach them. In his early twenties, he had come to live with his grandparents as a boy of seven in the mid-1920s when his father died down a local mine.

Widows lived in four of the 12 houses on Moxon's Yard. Three-generation families and extended families of uncles, aunts, and cousins lived under one roof or within a door or two of each other. Differences between the neighbors were few or were patched up quickly. There was little falling out with each other. They depended on each other, all believing that good neighbours were the best insurance policy they could have.

If William was outside, it was all but guaranteed that the children would play close to him. He had a way of making children feel listened to and valued. On many an evening he'd pull out a stool and sit outside the front door with the boys to discuss all manner of things about life with them. They knew they could ask William questions without fear of being told off for their curiosity or "not knowing their place." While in most households in Britain children were raised to believe that they were to be seen but not heard, that was not the case in the Bailey family. William was patient, kind, and genuinely interested in what the children had to say and wanted to know.

They sensed that, and, as a result, turned to him for wisdom and affirmation. He made them feel safe.

From time to time talk of work in the mines came up. It was the work that almost every man they knew did. With the exception of the teachers and shopkeepers they knew, it was the world they knew—their frame of reference for work in the world, for adulthood. They all clearly expected it to be their world in adulthood, too.

William had a clear opinion on that when it came to Harry's, Derek's, and Alan's futures. "Young Dek," he'd say to Derek with great seriousness during many a chat, "Tha's not going to work down the mine!" He meant it. He didn't want the boys to follow in his, their fathers', uncles', or grandfathers' footsteps to work in the pit. He wanted a better life and work for Harry and his friends. Derek would listen to William and think long and hard: If he didn't work down the pit, what else would he do? The steelworks, perhaps? It was hard to imagine anything else when all they knew, all they saw, all they heard about, all around them was connected to mining.

And when it came to conversations about Harry at home, William was clear on one thing with Edna, Harry's uncles and aunts, Nanan, and Grandfather Dyson: "We don't need more than one daft bugger working down the pit in this family."

William, 'though proud of the strength, toughness, and solidarity of miners, wanted to break the generation-to-generation cycle of all the men he knew—all the men everyone knew—of going down the pit. To him, it would be a dead end for the boys. He saw their intelligence and wanted something more for each of them. They were worth more than their physical strength and muscle being put to work scraping coal and a meager living underground. They were more than fodder for the pits.

When William witnessed Harry's intelligence, he thought back to his own intellectual and academic promise as a young boy. He did all he could to ensure that Harry could focus on learning. He didn't know how it would come about, but belief in something better for this newest generation of children became part of his being as a parent and friend to them. It had to start with telling them to think differently about their futures, to fan the flicker of the idea of something better into a bright flame in their minds.

Derek listened intently to William. Still, it was difficult to imagine a different world than the one he knew—unless, of course, he became a singing cowboy riding the range in the great expanse of the American West like Gene Autry or one of the many film stars the boys wanted to be like.

Carrying the Bat for Tommy Jacques

1939

Harry was cricket mad—like millions more boys in Britain and across the empire. And, like millions more, every chance they could, Harry and his friends went outside to "have a knock." Sometimes he, Derek, and Alan played. Other times they were joined by nearby Alfie Turton, choir friend John Turner, and cousins Ernest and Jack Payne. Lacking open green spaces, the boys improvised in creating their cricket pitch, chalking three vertical lines as wickets on the brick wall of the Regal. Harry was the one boy on Moxon's Yard who had a bat among the three boys living there, a sign of how scarce resources were for families on the yard. He mostly shared his bat well with his friends and between Moxon's Yard and the one small remaining field behind the Regal, play was lively, with each boy holding the image of one of their cricket heroes in their heads as they bowled and batted.

The Rawmarsh Cricket Club team was enjoying success, and their "star" player was none other than neighbor Tommy Jacques, 22, who lived at the top of Moxon's Yard. He made it a habit of playing a few rounds with the boys when he could—and he was generous in giving Harry and the other boys the much-coveted, collectible cricket hero cards from Player's Cigarette boxes he and his teammates amassed. Each year Player's produced 50 new cricket player cards, and the boys were as keen as any others in Britain to collect and trade cards toward the goal of a full set. Adding to the excitement, just two years earlier, the Yorkshire Cricket Club had won the 1937 County Championship.

Locally, the Rawmarsh Cricket Club off Barbers Lane was a popular destination for area families, during the longer, lighter spring and summer days. There was just one problem: Attending the matches was simply unaffordable to the Baileys. Harry missed out on seeing Tommy and the rest of the team play.

One day, Tommy, noticing Harry lingering outside to admire and see him go out in his cricket whites, sized up the situation and quickly came up with a solution. "Harry, it's a long way to the cricket pitch for me and I get tired even before I get there with all the walking. I'd be fine if carrying my bat didn't wear me out. Do you think you might help me by carrying my bat there for me so I can save my energy for the match? Of course, you'll need to stay for the whole match so you can help me carry my bat home."

At first Harry didn't know what to say. His heart leapt with happiness. Then he quickly replied, "Oh Tommy, let me just check with my mum. I can carry your bat for you if she says so!" Without wasting another moment, Harry sped down the yard to home, ran inside, and within a minute came out with Edna behind him. "My mum says yes!" Harry replied triumphantly. With that, Tommy Jacques handed his bat to Harry, who carried it proudly alongside his cricket hero neighbor. They walked along High Street past the Earl Grey to Rockliffe Road and a few streets more over to the Rawmarsh Cricket Club. Close to 300 spectators had gathered for the match. With Tommy Jacques at his side and a job to do, Harry needed no ticket to enter the cricket grounds. Instead, Tommy invited him to stay with the players and join them for tea. Harry was in heaven, enjoying the attention and the chance to see them play.

After the match, Tommy Jacques returned his bat to Harry once again to be carried home. Harry walked on air as they made their way along the streets toward Moxon's Yard and fans greeted them along the way.

"Well, then, Harry," said Tommy once they arrived at his doorstep, "You've done a cracking job carrying my bat for me today. Do you think you'd mind carrying my bat for me to my future matches?"

Harry's eyes lit up with excitement as he replied, "Oh Tommy, aye, that would be grand! Thank you!"

"Thank *you*, my young friend,' said Tommy with a wink and a friendly smile, "I'll depend on you to keep helping me, then, so I don't get worn out." He reached out to shake Harry's hand.

With that, Harry reverently passed Tommy's bat back to him and headed home happier than he could ever remember being.

And so Harry continued doing his special job for many years, carrying Tommy's bat to many more matches—staying and talking with the players he worshipped, the envy of his friends, enriched by the sense of doing something of value, and forever blessed by Tommy's kindness, a kindness he never forgot.

Tha's Not Going Up t' Tower

1939

At nine, Harry, with encouragement from Horace and Frank Pickering, began to take interest in a new role at St. Mary's in addition to being in the choir. He wanted to become a bell ringer, joining men and older boys in the art of change ringing. The bells were part of the heart and soul of Rawmarsh—sounding the time day after day, voicing the joys and sorrows of the community, calling parishioners to worship, holy days, and for wedding, funerals, and royal coronations.

Ringers performed a variety of changes—intricate, sequential, mathematical orderings of the sounding of the bells that relied heavily on teamwork among the ringers as they pulled ropes attached to bells mounted on wheels to sound the bells in the bell chamber above them.

The sound of the bells at St. Mary's had been a constant and comforting presence in Harry's life for as long as he could remember, and he first took closer notice of them when King George V died. In just under three hours on 28 January 1936, St. Mary's ringers performed a somber peal of Bob Major through 5,248 changes on muffled bells on the day of the king's funeral.

In happier circumstances, on May 12, 1937, Harry thoroughly enjoyed the mighty sounds of the ringers performing the same peal of Bob Major with the bells un-muffled to celebrate the coronation of King George VI and Queen Elizabeth.

Now nine, Harry became eager when Horace and Frank invited him for a visit up the bell tower—or campanile— accessed by a narrow spiraling stairwell of over 60 narrow steps. The climb up was well worth it; Harry was hooked after seeing the long ropes in the ringing chamber, then witnessing the ringers —mostly men and older boys who did double duty in the choir—pulling the ropes in sequence, led by a conductor.

Horace led Harry up on a ladder even higher into the bell chamber to see the bells hanging at the ready on their wheels—plus a few startled pigeons who nested there. Harry was eager to learn about the intricate changes.

The peal of eight bells made by John Taylor & Sons Foundry in Loughborough in 1917 was considered to be the finest in the West Riding. The bells had been transported to Rawmarsh first by rail, then on carts pulled by muscular draft horses up Rawmarsh Hill to St. Mary's. "Scientifically," said Frank Pickering to Horace and Harry with pride, "these bells were tuned to be pitch perfect. You won't find bells like these in Rotherham or Sheffield even, not even at the cathedral."

From "Plain Bob" to half and quarter peals, Harry had heard all manner of changes in his life but didn't know how the complex equations worked. Now, at nine, he was excited to think that the time had arrived that Frank Pickering and Horace thought he was big enough to ring, too. As Pickering told him, "It's more about concentration than strength, Harry, and you've got a mind for it. As long as you pay close attention to Horace and the others there's little that can go wrong."

After his exciting visit to the tower Harry rushed home to Edna and William, finding them sitting by the fireside with cups of tea in hand. He eagerly blurted out, "Mum! Dada! I'm going to join the ringers—ring the changes up the tower with Horace and the other ringers. He and Frank Pickering say I'm old enough now! They need more ringers and they asked *me*!"

William and Edna threw a quick glance at each other, then both frowned back at Harry.

His elation evaporated quickly as William said, "Tha's not going up t'tower my lad. Not on your life, son!"

Harry was startled. That was not at all the response he expected from his parents. They had never really discouraged him from an interest before. "But dada, why are you saying no? I don't understand," said Harry in a tone of mixed shock, disbelief, and indignation. "Why?" he said again, coming closer to his parents.

"Tha's not going to meet the same fate as your Nanan's grandpa," said William.

"Fate? What's fate? What fate?" asked a bewildered Harry.

"He died up in that bloody tower," William replied, speaking more forcefully than Harry could have expected. Even William was shocked by the force of his own response.

"Died? How? What do you mean?" said Harry. Edna put down the Hessian sack rug she was piecing together.

"Aye," William said. "Thomas Wilson, your great-great-grandad. His tombstone is alongside the church. No doubt you've walked by it—even played around it many a time—maybe even hid behind the stone to scare your mates. He was church warden like Frank Pickering is today. Like you he spent hours in and around the church. It was his life. So, as luck would have it the clock in the tower stopped working, stopped sounding the time. Everyone counted on that clock to know where to be and when, so it not sounding the time meant all manner of lateness and confusion. So, one day, after earlier attempts to fix it, Thomas and two labourers were sent up into the bell chamber to see what they could see in the hopes of fixing it. Lord knows what happened next, but one of the three took it upon himself to pull out some kind of pin in the clock mechanism in the ringing chamber. Next thing a weight smashed down from the bell chamber, breaking a beam, which then struck my great grandad's skull, crushing it partially. He was gravely wounded. They couldn't get him down to safety, so the local doctor and a surgeon from Rotherham were called to tend to him up in the bell chamber amidst the bell ropes and smashed beam. Thomas was right poorly and there was little that they could do for him. The doctors called for a mattress to be brought up. Imagine getting a mattress up all those winding narrow steps. They made the poor man as comfortable as they could. He died up there three days later."

Harry was both horrified and fascinated by the startling story—but also determined to ring. "Dada, that's a horrible thing, but I'm not afraid. I want to join the ringers! Please let me. Frank Pickering will be there. He's careful—and he said I'd be a fine ringer. Even Mr. Mortimer goes up the tower and he's even missing a leg!"

Edna put her sewing aside. "You heard your dada. Your Nanan will have a thing to two to say about it, too."

Harry's eyes flashed with confused anger. Then he decided to go straight to Nanan next door.

She was pleased as always to see Harry and welcomed him to sit with her and Uncle Leonard. She could see something was troubling him.

"Now then, Harry, you look right vexed. That's not like you. What's wrong?"

Harry sulked. Nanan and Leonard looked at each other, then back at Harry.

"Look here, Harry," said Leonard, "I've been collecting more Woodbines cards for you. Look—more cricketers for your collection, Take them, there's a good lad."

Harry took the cards from Leonard—but the dark cloud still hung over him as he briefly looked at the cricketers on the cards. Normally he would have been happy to have more to add to his collection, but not today. "Ta," said Harry unenthusiastically.

"Go on, then lad," said Nanan, "Has the cat caught your tongue then?" She smiled.

Harry looked down, then after a minute began, "My dada says no to me being a bell ringer at church even though I'm ready and they need ringers. Dada says it's because your great grandad died in the tower."

"Lord!" said Nanan, "I haven't thought about that in donkey's years. I must have told your dada about it years ago. Yes, my dad's grandad died a terrible death up in that tower, poor man. There was even an inquest—a hearing about it. Dreadful business. So very sad."

"But Nanan," said Harry, "I know that's a terrible thing, but I want to ring, and mum and dada say not on my life!"

Nanan couldn't help but smile at Harry's seriousness. She patted his arm and said, "You are your mum's and dada's only child. They love you and want what's best for you. They don't want what befell poor old Thomas Wilson to happen to you."

"But Nanan, I won't come to any harm. The bells are rung all the time and I know they are taken care of. Horace Bailey will be there. He's not daft. We'll be careful."

Uncle Leonard lit up a cigarette, took a slow drag on it, surveyed his nephew, then flicked the ash into the hearth and said, "It sounds to me like you want your Nanan to have a word with your dad about this."

Harry nodded his head up and down seriously. "I want to ring—and I won't die up there." Nanan listened to his plaintive yet resolute tone and couldn't help but smile at the seriousness on his face.

"Right, lad. You give me some time and we'll set this straight. I don't want another family member to meet a nasty end in that tower, but my guess is that as long as you are willing to listen carefully to Frank Pickering and Horace Bailey and the other ringers and learn, you'll be a champion ringer and do my great granddad proud."

Harry brightened and looked up appreciatively at Nanan. "Yes, I will listen and learn. I will be ever so careful."

"Right then, lamb. I'll talk with your parents. Maybe Frank Pickering can put a word in for you, too."

"Oh Nanan, thank you!" said Harry, giving her a hug, "That will be grand!"

After that Harry and Uncle Leonard went out to the front steps where the light was better to look at the Woodbines cards. Before too long Harry was ready to go home again, knowing that if Nanan said she'd put in a word for him she'd be true to her word. He could always count on Nanan.

A few days later, Harry was up in the tower alongside Horace learning the ropes and watching how the experienced ringers worked together to ring the intricate changes that set the bells into motion and filled the valley with the sounds of St. Mary's bells. It felt like heaven to him.

Willam Henry Bailey, age 23, and *Edna Dyson,* age 22, 1924: *A visit to the Scarborough seaside and dressed in their Sunday Best. William and Edna wed in August 1925. Harry was born in 1930.*

Harry as a toddler, about age 2, circa 1932:
This blurry image is the first from his childhood.

Harry (age 4), his parents, and Grandfather Dyson and Emily Pierce: *Taken at Blackpool, August 1934, just before Edna's 32nd birthday. Photographed by "Dennis R. Thompson, Photographic Artist"*

"Little Harry" as pageboy and cousin Audrey Astbury as flower girl as his Uncle Rowland Dyson wed Eva Talbot (upper left). Cousin Katie Astbury stands by the bride. April 1938, St. Mary Magdalene's, Whiston Parish Church, Yorkshire.

SCHOOL·DAYS
1941

Harry, age 11, in his Rawmarsh school uniform, 1941.
It is the only wartime photo we have of him.

Examination Results, Session 1947-48

OPEN EXHIBITION IN ENGLISH.
Edward J. Hughes at Pembroke College, Cambridge.

OPEN EXHIBITION IN NATURAL SCIENCE.
Norman R. Large at Exeter College, Oxford.

STATE SCHOLARSHIPS.
Norman R. Large at Exeter College, Oxford.
Roy Nicholls at the University, Birmingham.

W.R.C.C. MAJOR SCHOLARSHIPS.
John D. Golicher, Vl.A.Sc., at the University, Nottingham.
Dennis J. Hatfield, Vl.A.Sc., at the University, Sheffield.
Norman R. Large, Vl.A.Sc., at the University, Oxford.
Roy Nicholls, Vl.A.Sc., at the University, Birmingham.
Jack Wadsworth, Vl.A.Sc., at the University, Leeds.
Harold Blakemore, Vl.A.Arts, at the University College, London.
Brian O'Malley, Vl.A.Arts, at the University, Manchester.

W.R.C.C. MUSIC SCHOLARSHIP.
Dorothy Willoughby, Vl.A.Arts, at the Royal Academy.

W.R.C.C. EXHIBITION.
Margaret Fanshaw, Vl.A.Arts.

HIGHER SCHOOL CERTIFICATE RESULTS.
(Small letters indicate Distinction in Principal Papers. Capital letters indicate Excellence in Scholarship Papers. C, c (*Chemistry*); Z (*Zoology*); m (*Maths.*); p (*Physics*); e (*English*); g (*Geography*); H, h (*History*); A (*Arts*); F (*French*).

FORM VI.A SCIENCE.

Boys: Bailey, H.
Bell, C. H.
Brown, A.
Burley, D. (s).
Coop, W.
Golicher, J. D. (Z.).
Hatfield, D. (m. c.).

Hughes, E. S.
Large, N. R. (m. p. c.).
Nicholls, R. (C, c. p.).
Shaw, F.
Wadsworth, J. (c.).
Wild, E. H.
Woods, K.

Girls: Green, Suzanne.

FORM VI.A ARTS.

Boys: Blakemore, H. (e. h.).
Hadkins, F.
Hughes, E. J. (g.).

Mirfin, H.
O'Malley, B. (H. h.).

Girls: Birdsall, Megan
Brewster, Mabel
Duffield, Sylvia
Fanshaw, Dorothy (f).
Hamstead, Rachel

Hepworth, Edith
Sanders, Patricia
Steer, Gertrude
Whiteside, Audrey
Willoughby, Dorothy

LETTERS OF SUCCESS.
(Capital Letters indicate passes in Principal Subjects, and small letters indicate pass at Subsidiary Standard. p. (*Physics*); m. (*Maths.*); e. (*English Literature*); el. (*English Language*); f. (*French*); hc. (*Handicraft*); ph. (*Physiology and Hygiene*); d. (*Art*); g. (*Geog.*); b. (*Biology*); c. (*Chemistry*); h. (*History*); x (*Scripture*); am. (*Applied Maths.*).

FORM VI.A.

Boys: Burton, M. (M. C. e.)
Goulty, V. (M. c.).
Hayhurst, G. (G. c. el.).

Marshall, A. (C. B.).
Willis, B. (m. P.).
Shephard, M. (e. H. D.).

Girls: Bucknell, M. (E, g, F.)
Riley, Sheila (e. d.).

Ward, Eileen (G. d.).
Whitfield, Joyce (E. H. f.).

FORM VI.B.

Boys: Boulton, J. (am.).
Holmes, P. (am.).

Nettleton, K. (c. el.).
Wood, A. (c.).

FORM VI GENERAL.

Boys: Brown, D. (el. h. g. f.).
Lilley, B. (e. f.).

Shaw, D. (e. h. f.).
Swift, G. (el. e. g. ph.).

Girls: Brown, Barbara (el. d.).
Booth, Constance (d.).
Clare, Audrey (cl.).
Clarkson, Iris (el. e. h. g. ph.).
Corbridge, Betty (el. d. x.).
Downing, Jean (e. g. ph.).
Dyson, Jean (e. el. ph.).
Fletcher, Greta (e. ph.).
Ingham, Betty (el. ph.).

Lindley, Charlotte (d.).
Liversidge, Vera (x, ph.).
Short, Joyce, (d. ph.).
Stables, Ann (d. ph.).
Taylor, Marie (h. ph.),
Thompson, Kathleen (g. ph.).
Wilkinson, Mary (d.).
Winter, Joyce (el. e. ph.).

Mexborough Grammar School
Advanced Level Examination Results, 1947-1948.
Harry is listed among students earning their
Higher School Certificate for Science.

215

St. Mary's Parish Church, Rawmarsh, Rotherham. Later in life Harry reminisced about how much time he spent there in his youth, "up, in, and around" the family's long-time parish church. Harry blossomed there and formed important friendships as a choir boy, bell ringer, Sunday school student, youth group member, and Boy Scout.

St. Mary's baptismal font, where Edna and William asserted that "Harry" was a proper name.

216

Diane Bailey-Boulet, *the author, standing at the St. Mary's altar, 2004, during her first return visit there since a brief one as a 9-year-old in 1970.*

(Above) Diane Bailey-Boulet with Horace Bailey, Harry's closest friend, mentor, and co-conspirator: Standing at the St. Mary's altar beside the choir stalls and organ. Horace stayed connected to St. Mary's into his 90s

(Left) Horace and Diane stand at the site of Harry's Moxon's Yard front door. The Regal Cinema building stands in the background. Moxon's Yard was demolished in 1969. The Regal, built in 1931 during cinema's heyday, became a casino and bingo hall by the 1960s. By 2004 its backside was a Netto discount shop. The building was demolished in 2013. A newer retail block stands there today, including a Tesco Express.

Anderson Shelter

1939

In 1939, across Britain, families prepared for the growing specter of a new kind of warfare, one where attacks on civilians and industry would be the horrifying new norm, not a side effect of war. Nazi Germany had built a war machine unlike anything seen elsewhere, directing their resources to building bombers capable of penetrating British airspace, tanks that rolled invincibly across Europe into country after country to dominate and force surrender, and battle ships and submarines capable of disrupting shipping lines and the cargo that Britain so depended on for its food supply and economy centered on global trade.

The mines, steel works, and rail lines that filled almost every mile in and between Sheffield, Rotherham, and Rawmarsh were critical—from munitions manufacture to rolling out specialty steel for aircraft. They were obvious bombing targets. To the west, Manchester, Leeds, Blackpool, and Liverpool were clear targets.

In an ominous sign of the looming threat of war, kits to build Anderson Shelters—designed to protect families from bombings—were made available to families across Britain. The shelters were distributed at no cost to poor families.

The shelters could hold six people. William, Edna, and Harry were to share theirs in a tight squeeze with Nanan, Leonard. The Coopers built one close by. Each shelter was made of six pieces of corrugated steel, to be constructed at the back of the house. The first step in the construction was digging deep ditches before bolting together of the pieces to build each curve-shaped shelter. Neighbors up and down the yard helped each other assemble them. William, Leonard, and Arthur Cooper worked together to dig their needed ditches, then assemble the shelters that would protect their two families.

The boys helped their dads, carrying away the displaced dirt and stones and dumping them at the end of Moxon's Yard, where an area was simultaneously being excavated by the local council for a water storage tank in case it was needed for extinguishing fires from bombing attacks.

All the digging revealed something of Moxon's Yard's past: Harry and Derek spotted and retrieved broken shards of pottery in the dirt. Moxon's Yard had been the site of one of Rawmarsh's potteries in previous centuries.

And as the males in the family dug and hauled dirt, Edna, Nanan, and Mary Ellen planned for the shelter interiors. They would need bunks to sleep on, if that was possible when under threat of attack. They also focused on food—the preparation, production, and preservation of it. Food would be a critical part of winning any war.

After the work of bolting the pieces of the Anderson Shelter was done, everyone pitched in to fill sandbags for the outside and to cover the corrugated steel shelter with dirt as directed—an extra layer of protection. Next the families filled the shelter with benches, blankets, a kerosene lamp, matches, bottled water, tins of sardines, and other food they might need if they were in the shelter for a long time. Edna had recently pieced together a rug with old blanket pieces and Hessian sack, so she brought it out to put on the shelter floor. And while the middens were just beyond, including a chamber pot in the shelter was still essential if the call of nature happened as bombs dropped down on them.

Space would be a tight in the shelters. The boys gathered small games to play to while away the time should there be longs hours spent inside the shelter's walls—cards, marbles, Woodbines Cigarettes cricket player cards they'd collected and traded. Harry brought in his Boy Scouts guidebook and a crossword puzzle book with sharpened pencils that Auntie Kath had given him at his previous birthday. Nanan had Harry post a picture of King George, Queen Elizabeth, and the Princesses Elizabeth and Margaret Rose on the wall when everything else was done. With the shelters built, furnished, and "decorated" neighbors up and down Moxon's Yard gave each other tours of their shelters, just as millions more families across Britain did. It was a strangely light-hearted experience while, just inside their kitchen back doors, everyone kept their gas masks on hooks so they could be grabbed and worn if attacked.

At schools, offices, and factories across the land, everyone began to become familiar with the low rising, then steady constant high pitch of air raid sirens. The children drilled at school every other day for 20 minutes, heading to bomb shelters built below playing fields with their goggle-eyed gasmasks. The sickly strong smell of rubber made wearing the masks all the more challenging while practicing sitting in neat rows on benches.

As summer came, the Baileys joined many millions more in taking a seaside holiday: It was the first year the miners were given paid holiday time. The seaside communities with their long piers and streets full of narrow boarding houses were busier than ever. Everyone wanted to make the most of it—to cling to peacetime and warm weather.

William, Edna, and Harry joined the crowds headed to Blackpool on the Irish Sea, walking the broad promenade, passing the Woolworth's that had enough dining space for 2000 people, hoping to be able to afford tickets to a performance at the Winter Garden, making their way past the famous ball rooms with elegant women and men in their gowns and tuxedoes. Harry was in awe of massive sights of Blackpool Tower and the famous Ferris wheel.

Gazing out at high or low tide into the Irish Sea they could see an engineering feat of another kind: Protective barriers newly built to repel German amphibious attack. Seaside playground aside, Blackpool, too, was preparing for war. It was now a training center for the armed forces.

August 1939 was the most bittersweet of summers. William and Edna, married fourteen years earlier in the same month, thought of the times they had visited Blackpool together when they first met in their mid-20s in the mid-1920s, when they had laughed, danced, and gazed at the same sea surrounded by the same sights and dreamt of a bright future together. Life had so often been a struggle since then. Now all they could do is be brave and do their best to live with courage so that Harry could, too. They did their best to put on a brave face, to make the most of where they were now.

Not burdened with the same sad memories of a tragic First World War or dread of what might come as his parents, Harry breathed in the briny, warm salt air and watched the waves lap the shores as he listened to the seagulls overhead. Soon the three walked on. William let Harry pick out a sweet coloured stick of Blackpool rock. Harry laughed, thinking that there was nothing sweet about Mr. Cater's infamous black "rock" cane back at Dale Road School. They stopped by a seafood stall for a pot of sweet, yet briny cockles William enjoyed with a good sprinkling of vinegar.

Soon they joined with thousands more in sitting on canvas striped chairs on the beach. William then queued with Harry so he could go on a donkey ride. Later, they joined a crowd and laughed at a Punch & Judy Show. In the evening after tea the three enjoyed the arcades and rides and the famous Blackpool illuminations.

Despite the festive air, the headlines on signs outside all the newsagents' shops shared the same bad news: Nazi Germany, all but invincible, was continuing its onslaught in Europe. Prime Minister Baldwin's hope that Hitler would seek peace was evaporating. Britain could not stand idly by as Poland and all of Europe were trampled by a despot. As the darkness closed in, Harry, Edna, William and all the thousands of Blackpool holidaymakers individually and collectively focused on every precious moment, every breeze, every seagull's high-pitched cry, every wave lapping the sceptr'd isle, every happy squeal of children on the amusement rides, every braying donkey. The sound of buoyant dance hall and vaudeville music carried through the air.

When at last the Baileys boarded the train to return home, their climb up the steps into the carriage was a reluctant one. The bags they carried to Blackpool had more weight than they remembered. Edna rustled deep into her purse to find a small bag of sweets, offering one each to William and Harry. And as the conductor finally whistled its departure, the train lumbered and rumbled down the tracks. Harry craned his neck to look backward at the Blackpool lights for as long as he could, until he lost sight of them and the nightfall signaling the end of their holiday closed in. He leaned his head against William's shoulder and fell asleep.

On 1 September, soon after returning home, the crisis with Germany had worsened further. While not yet at war, the Air Ministry announced new blackout regulations, intent on reducing visibility to man-made light that could aid enemy aircraft in navigating over Britain. On Moxon's Yard as across Britain, everyone followed the order to hang blackout curtains over all windows and doors to the outside—or fill windows with paint or cardboard if necessary—before sunset each night. The Baileys took the heavy black felt made available to them as part of the regulation and attached the large fabric onto pieces of timber to hang on the windows and over the doors onto Moxon's Yard and to the back of the house. Not a speck of light or a glow of any sort could be seen from the outdoors. Newly appointed civilian Air Raid Precaution Wardens had the power to levy strict penalties if they spotted even the slightest bit of light. They saw to it that every household and business followed the orders. All businesses, mines, and factories were also included.

Streetlights were turned off. The valleys were not visible once the sun went down. High Street went dark—and any motors cars, trams, or lorries on them had to be dark and their headlights covered partially, as if eye lids were added to them, so light could only glow downward. Moxon's Yard—like all of Britain—became suddenly a much darker place at night. The marquee of the Regal went dark.

Lights needed to be turned off before opening and closing doors. William, Edna, and Harry followed the guidance to affix tape to their windows to reduce damage and injury from shattered glass from possible air raids. All they could do now was hope that against the odds peace would come. But if it didn't, they were as prepared as they knew how to be.

"This country is now at war with Germany"

3 September 1939 – Sunday

"Jerusalem, my happy home
When shall I come to thee?
When shall my sorrows have an end?
Thy joys when shall I see?
O happy harbor of the saints!
O sweet and pleasant soil!
In thee no sorrow may be found,
No grief, no care, no toil."

It was the 15th Sunday after Trinity. A beautiful, sunny, almost balmy day. The candles on the altar of St. Mary's flickered brightly, much as flames of light had flickered for at least as long as the almost 900 years since the church structure was first recorded as being on that hilly site in the *Domesday Book* published at the order of William the Conqueror in 1086 to survey the whole of the land he had overwhelmed twenty years earlier.

229

Now brilliant sunlight illuminated the stained glass windows and the great bells had stopped reverberating after the ringers dropped their ropes and made their way downstairs to join the service. It was past time for the 11:00 morning service to begin—but it was instead delayed. In homes across Britain including the rectory across the street and the Coopers' house, Britons heard Prime Minister Chamberlain announce on the wireless the dreaded news that everyone had expected: "This country is at war with Germany." Fulfilling its treaty commitment, Britain declared war in response to Germany's invasion of Poland.

When Rev. Scovell at last ascended to the pulpit he looked grave, resolute, and somehow aged in an instant. He quietly surveyed the faces before him—seeming to lock into every face—young, old, men, women, and children—as if concentrating so he could capture an image of each person in that moment. Not a one would be spared from fear or anguish in what was to come. He then took in a long, deep breath. Leaning forward against the lectern, in a measured voice, he repeated Prime Minister Neville Chamberlain's words, saying with firmness of voice and with great sadness that "The long struggle to win the peace had failed."

Though its aisles were full of worshippers, St. Mary's was silent, but for the aggressive sound outside of large black crows perched on tombstones outside *caw-caw-cawing* in the late morning sun.

It wouldn't be long before the sounds of air raid sirens would echo across the Rother Valley. With war declared, it was entirely possible that attacks by air could begin to hit Britain that very day. While war had been expected, the news still hit hard. Everyone had hoped upon hope that Hitler would prove to be as committed to avoiding war as Chamberlain. The opposite was true. The clarity of this reality was chilling. Now everyone had a grim certainty to work with in their individual and collective minds.

As Nanan looked toward the choir at the young men in their purple choir robes, ruffled white collars, and white cassocks, she thought back to young men and boys like them she had known a generation earlier who had stood in the very same places before the Great War: Young men who went off to war as soldiers and sailors, some of whom did not return, or, if they did, returned damaged in mind and spirit. She could still remember their faces. She looked over at Frank Pickering.

She had known him when he was a young lad before he and many more like him went off to fight and endure the horrors of the Great War. Boys her daughters went to school with and just that bit older than William. She thought of Harry Mortimer, who had lost his leg to war, and Cuffty Barrow, who, after losing an arm in the war and returning to a land "Fit for Heroes", was now doing a job the council had offered him sweeping Rawmarsh's streets using the one arm he still had. She thought of her own son William, still a boy, whose opportunities and horizons narrowed with war and the day he left school in 1915 to proudly work in the mines alongside his father, uncles, and neighbors to fuel the war effort. Around her in the church were men and women whose lives had already been forever altered by the brutality of war, lost in hellish battles at Verdun and the Somme—and the massive, unprecedented carnage and devastation it exacted on a generation.

All but the youngest adults present at church that morning had lived through the Great War. Many remembered losing sons or whole villages of fathers, sons, uncles, brothers, friends in Pals Battalions slaughtered together in brutal trench battles at the Somme and Verdun. Wound infections, lost limbs, lost sanity, disease were added tragedies. No one had lived through it unscathed. Women had lost the loves of their lives, fiancés, husbands, sons, brothers, cousins, and sweethearts. Twenty-one years on many remained unmarried and without mates. The deadly wave of Spanish Influenza that followed the Great War ensured that much of the flower of England—as elsewhere—had been lost. Now this next generation of young people would face a ruthless enemy in a new age of technologically advanced warfare targeting civilians. Everyone's life would once again somehow be touched by the loss, death, fear, and pain. There was no way out, only through, what was to come.

Harry looked over at Nanan, sitting in her usual pew, and saw she was pale, with a stricken expression. She must have sensed he was looking at her. She looked up to the altar at Harry, Horace, Norman, and all the young men in the choir. Some would soon join the armed forces far from all they knew. She caught the eye of one of Harry's male teachers, who would undoubtedly be quickly called up to war. She looked at one stricken face after another. She thought of all her grandchildren—Ernest, Jack, Harry, Dennis. All so young and full of promise. Tears filled her eyes as she squeezed her

233

fingers open and shut against her palms repeatedly and dug deep within herself to maintain her composure. She thought back to her own childhood—when only horses, trains, and canal boats moved people. It was almost an entirely different world. Aeroplanes were all but unimaginable, never mind ones that dropped bombs on town and countryside alike. She knew that no one would be untouched by a war with the real possibility of mass chemical attacks. How long would this war go on? Would Britain win or be conquered? Would her daughters, sons, grandsons, granddaughters, nieces and nephews live to be free men and women? There was no knowing.

The silent knowing that enveloped the adults in the sanctuary now was one of collective knowing that victory would be hard-fought-for and exact a terrible cost, a cost that had to be born to ensure a Britain, an empire, and world free of Hitler's boundless and bloodthirsty cruelty. As sun streamed in through the windows, the silence spoke volumes where words were inadequate to express the tragedy of it all. There was a collective sense of heightened reverence for the lives of the younger generations present, who would fight the fight and whose youth and innocence would be sacrificed under the darkest of shadows. Where everyone cheerily expected the Great War to be "over in two weeks" in 1914, there were no such illusions now in 1939 that war would be anything but brutal, long, and painful. The seemingly invincible Nazi war machine would now unleash its furies on Britain. It was time to draw on the deepest resolve, ingenuity, and reserves of courage and resilience to overcome this enemy's seeming invincibility.

Everyone present in St. Mary's that morning experienced an unsettling paradox of feelings: They were keenly aware of everything around them, every hymn and anthem sung, every creaking of the wooden pews, every vibration of the organ, as if trying to rivet a memory to their minds of these final remnants of peace, yet their focus was also equally elsewhere, as each person in his or her own way tried to make sense of the wider world darkening and closing in on and around them.

Harry looked out at the congregation from the altar, seeing a grief on the faces of the people unlike any he had witnessed before. Old people looked older, and all the parents he knew, both his own and those of his friends and school mates, looked suddenly fragile, and in all cases all-too-knowing that what lay in front of them, in front of their nation, made it an absolute duty to fight for a future free of the worst of tyrannies. Harry looked to Horace for clues on what he was thinking and saw his intense intelligence animating his features as he made his own mental calculations of what was to come. Harry's knees began to tremble beneath his choir robe, only worsening as he tried to stop it. The day everyone dreaded and prepared for had come. Now it was time to muster all the bravery and resilience they could.

Abide with me: fast falls the eventide;
the darkness deepens; Lord, with me abide.
When other helpers fail and comforts flee,
Help of the helpless, O abide with me.
Swift to its close ebbs out life's little day;
earth's joys grow dim, its glories pass away.
Change and decay in all around I see.
O Lord who changes not, abide with me.
I need your presence every passing hour.
What but your grace can foil the tempter's power?
Who like yourself my guide and strength can be?
Through cloud and sunshine, O abide with me.
I fear no foe with you at hand to bless,
though ills have weight, and tears their bitterness.
Where is death's sting? Where, grave, your victory?
I triumph still, if you abide with me.

Hold now your Word before my closing eyes.
Shine through the gloom and point me to the skies.
Heaven's morning breaks and earth's vain shadows
flee;
in life, in death, O Lord, abide with me.
--Henry Francis Lyte

A Different Kind of Education

September 1939

Harry had been due to return to school with all his friends from summer holiday, but an almost immediate result of the war was that some of the male teachers at school were called up for military service and the re-opening of school was postponed. It was closer to Christmas when everyone settled into a more normal school routine. But normal it was not. There were new teachers at Haugh Road School: retired women and young women, many just out of college who were recruited straight fresh from their own classrooms to teach.

The sound of air raid sirens became a steady presence in day-to-day life. Night in the shelter became the uncomfortable, nerve-wracking norm. Some days at school very few children or teachers were present: If there had been an air raid warning with sirens the night before, school was not obligatory. Edna, however, made a point of sending Harry to school whenever possible. It alarmed her that the war was disruptive of Harry's education.

Still there were nights when nobody slept well and where fear had exacerbated exhaustion. The blasting of the "Big Bertha" anti-aircraft *ack-ack* guns and the roar of enemy and friendly aircraft engines echoed thought the valleys and in between.

Sometimes it was enough for Harry to go to school and simply play football or other games with students who were there.

Then one night after an air raid, news spread throughout Rawmarsh that a German bomber had been hit and crashed somewhere in nearby Hooton Roberts. Many of the older children hopped on bicycles and rode there hoping to see it. Edna and Mary Ellen Cooper refused to let Harry, Derek, and Alan go. They were simply too young. The children who did ride there were turned back by the army, which had cordoned off the crash site.

The big alarm mixed with excitement between Rawmarsh and Hooton Roberts was that the German crew was not found with their plane. They had to have bailed out and were hiding somewhere. It became the job of the police to go from village to village and to each shop, school, factory, and pit to try to find them.

Cousins Ernest and Jack were the ones to triumphantly announce the big excitement to the family: The crew had been found at Haugh Road School—hiding in a bomb shelter. A miner on his way to work early in the morning had spotted somebody harvesting turnips in the field nearby.

Jack and Ernest were among the students at school when a Black Maria van arrived and soldiers began pouring out of it, racing toward the school's air raid shelters.

Before long two Germans were running away from the shelter into the playing fields. One headed toward the girls' school but made an especially poor choice of which door to enter in his attempt to escape. He found himself in the school kitchens, where the head cook was already at work wielding a meat cleaver, about to chop meat for the day's lunch. Before long the prisoner was handed over to the army police. The other German crew member had already been rounded up.

News spread quickly that the prisoners had been spotted. Dozens of housewives grabbed their rolling pins and kitchen knives, poured out of their houses, and raced to Haugh Road to take on the unwelcome visitors and protect their children. It was all the army police could do to keep them at bay so they would not harm the captured Germans.

The War Takes Its Toll

1940

Air-raid sirens sounded immediately across Britain with the declaration of war on 3 September 1939—but no air attacks came. From September to October through December, then into the new year and early spring of 1940 there was no sign of the Luftwaffe. Many began to call it the Phoney War. It was tempting to become complacent. The Ministry of Home Security had to start a poster campaign to remind everyone to still carry their gas masks: "Hitler will send no warning—so always carry your gas masks."

In the Rother Valley, army barracks and a barrage balloon station were in place on Greasbro' Tops along with anti-aircraft guns, which everyone called *Big Berthas*. Powerful search lights positioned there met up with the beams of ones in Thrybergh, three miles southeast of Rawmarsh to detect incoming Nazi bombers. German bombers would inevitably strike close by. Given the importance of the coal, steel, and other industries essential to the war effort, Sheffield,

Rotherham, and Parkgate would be attractive targets at any time. Leeds, Manchester, and Liverpool to the west were also obvious targets.

Almost out of the blue, in May 1940, the first air attack of the war on British soil struck North Yorkshire, just 90 miles from Rawmarsh. A single German bomber dropped its payload of 13 bombs on Middlesbrough, an industrial town with a large steelworks. The North Sea that Harry had enjoyed in his visits to Scarborough and Whitby was now the Luftwaffe's clear path from Europe to England.

The Baileys and Coopers were as prepared as they could be for nights in their shared Anderson Shelter, with William and Leonard in charge of fire watching during an air raid. They made sure that buckets set outside the back doors were full of water to help extinguish flames or smoldering materials. Harry, Derek, and Alan helped fill the buckets alongside their dads.

The first nights in the shelter were naturally frightening, when the sirens that warned of an incoming raid interrupted their fitful sleep. There was little room in the crowded shelters the families sought refuge in. Nanan's arthritis made it especially difficult for her to get into and out of the shelter. But everyone helped each other. William, with his gift for making children feel safe and valued, made the boys feel more at ease, telling them stories that made them laugh as a kerosene lamp glowed, lighting up their faces in the small space. It almost felt like Boy Scouts camp.

By June, convoys in the English Channel, London, and South Wales were under attack. The brutal bombing of London—the Blitz—continued all summer into September. The capital was badly damaged with much loss of life, but its residents, among them Prime Minister Churchill, were resolute in carrying on. The pilots of the Royal Air Force—flying Spitfire and Hawker Hurricane aircraft—took to the skies again and again as the nimble line of defence for the nation.

As the RAF sparred with the Luftwaffe overhead month after month, Edna joined with housewives up and down the British Isles, when called to do so, gladly gathering and turning over her one aluminum cooking pot so that the much-needed metal could be turned into more Spitfires and

Hurricanes for the RAF. It was vital to the war effort to replace those shot down in the Battle of Britain and build even more.

In June, as the Blitz was in full force in London, word came over the wireless that bells in churches and chapels across the nation must not be rung. Bells in Britain were now only to be rung on the directions of the higher authorities as a warning of attacks from the air by German armed forces. This silenced bells that had, in many cases, rung for centuries without disruption. The tower at St. Mary's fell quiet but for the cooing and rustling of the now undisturbed pigeons who nested there. Two weeks after the decree silenced the bells, France surrendered to the Nazis.

With the late summer of 1940, a near relentless assault on Liverpool meant that Luftwaffe bombers began to menace the West Riding on their way to bomb the strategically important port and docks of this shipping gateway to North America. In late August, 160 bombers attacked Liverpool and continued to do so for three nights straight, then with regularity over three more months. The Luftwaffe attacked Liverpool 50 times in three months. At its worst, 300 bombers struck the port city, striking part of the city's almost new cathedral.

The cities of Bradford and Leeds were also bombed in August 1940, too, and random bombings struck parts of the West Riding.

After the challenges of the spring and summer, in October 1940, Harry peered out the window that was covered with crisscrosses of sticky paper to prevent possible shattering of glass from Luftwaffe bombing attacks everyone dreaded. The pattern almost looked like the Union Jack.

Over a year had passed since the war began, the family had spent many nights in the Anderson Shelters with Nanan and the Coopers. They were all tired and achy from the cramped conditions but work and living had to go on despite the fear that permeated everyone's lives. They were now long since used to the signs posted at the Regal urging patrons to bring their gas masks to the cinema with them in case of an attack.

Following the Ministry of Defence guidance to households across the land, the families on Moxon's Yard made sure every window was reinforced with sticky paper to hopeful reduce shattering. Each household mounted timbers with black felt as blackout curtains so that "not a speck of light" could be seen from them when nightfall came, and lights were on inside. Air Raid Precaution Wardens made their way up and down the streets and yards with row-upon-row of terraced houses to make sure residents took this seriously. Word got out fast when a household was warned to be more careful, or fined. One woman in Rawmarsh was fined heavily when her cat pushed the blackout curtain aside while she was not home, making the light inside the house visible. It became second nature to turn lights off before opening a door to go out at night.

Still, the business of life had to go on. Everyone had lives to live the best they could, war or no war. The miners and steelworkers had more work to do than ever, whether they had slept well the night before or not. The women at home still had their many chores to do to manage their households, plus in many cases even more work as men in their families enlisted in the armed forces and headed to their posts. Young women still at home filled the factories to make the needed weapons and supplies of war—and did what had formerly been "men's work" to support the war effort.

The stakes were enormous. Harry, Edna, and William could see what everyone talked about and saw in the newspapers, heard on the wireless, and watched on the cinema news reels both leading up to and after Britain entered the war: Hitler's merciless machine was advancing in all directions across Europe and on the high seas. The nation's supply of food and other necessities was starkly reduced as ships were sunk or unable to make it safely to port from the colonies and trading partners that Britain had become dependent on. Britain was largely on its own.

Gone were the oranges Harry and his friends got at penny rush at Robbie's Cinema in exchange for bringing a jar. Fred Whitlam shuttered his fish & chips shop when fishing fleets were in too much danger to go to sea and the potatoes and cooking oil to make the chips were rationed and in short supply. The rabbit meat he sold each Thursday and which Edna made into a much-enjoyed stew at home was now a thing of the past. Some of the deprivations of war were almost immediate, others came in gradually.

Now, as Harry looked pensively outside, he watched as the sheets and towels Edna had hung flapped, rose, and fell again with the gusts of cold wind that swept across Rawmarsh. Wrapped up in a patched cardigan to cut the chill, Edna was outside below, scrubbing at something Harry couldn't make out, but doing so with grim determination. She looked worn and pale, even more so than normal. And after days of the usual working, cleaning, and cooking, the Baileys, Nanan, Uncle Leonard, and the Coopers all prepared for bedtime knowing that their rest could well be interrupted by the swelling sound, then blaring of air raid sirens and the subsequent need to seek shelter together quickly in the cramped, often damp shelter.

While sirens had sounded several nights, so far, the West Riding had been spared. It was a matter of time before it was their turn to face the ominous droning sound of scores of Messerschmitt and Junkers bombers. The threat of the far-more-menacing modern air attack made Edna wonder how and whether they would survive. If they did, would it be because they were all to be enslaved by the Nazis? Would Harry, Derek, Alan, Horace and nephews Jack and Ernest be dragged away as fodder for the Nazi machine? What of Irene, Dorothy, Elsie, and Audrey? This was no way for children to live and grow up. In these moments when fear was the all too constant companion, Edna, like millions more, dug in deep within to take to heart the words of Prime Minister Churchill's June speech during the Battle of Britain, "Let us therefore brace ourselves to our duties and so bear ourselves that, if the British Empire and its Commonwealth last a thousand years, men will still say '*This was their finest hour.*'"

Bringing herself back to the present moment, where peace was behind them and the war's brutality yet to reach them directly, Edna finished her scrubbing and, as she rose and turned to re-enter the house, noticed Harry looking down at her from his bedroom window. She smiled weakly, then went inside and called upstairs to him, "Your Auntie Nellie is coming by tomorrow for a cup of tea!"

"All right mum," Harry replied, the first words he had spoken in over two hours. Auntie Nellie always brought a different perspective on life in her visits. She was spirited, snobbish, opinionated, better off, and saw herself as a cut above her sisters and made sure they knew it. Somehow, to Harry, she was also always a source of amusement and interest for him. He enjoyed her visits, if only because she looked at life in many ways so differently from her younger sisters. There was nothing sedate about her.

When Nellie arrived the next day for tea, she did so with as much ceremony as she could muster, perhaps fancying herself to be more like the queen or a great lady. She was always one to have grand ideas, at least as her sisters Edna and Elsie saw it. Even more than Edna, she frequently reminded anyone in earshot that, "My mother was a lady…" and fashioned herself on how she imagined her mother would have. She arrived at the door with a nice hat and gloves on.

Always forthright, upon stepping inside, Nellie took one look at her exhausted sister and scrawny nephew, declaring, "Oh you do look worn out, you do!" Edna didn't know what to say, and Harry was just as speechless. "Come, this won't do," continued Nellie. "You are in need of a rest. Next weekend you pack up your things and come stay overnight with me. I'll see to it that you put your feet up and get some energy back. As is, you look a right mess."

Edna never quite knew what to say when her elder sister dished out her recipe mixing gracious invitation, snobbery, and insult. But she did know that Nellie kept a fine home and garden on Doncaster Place in Rotherham. An overnight there would be a nice break from Moxon's Yard. "Right then, Nellie," Edna replied, "We'll be glad to visit you. Ta—that is—thank you."

The following Friday afternoon, Edna, William, and Harry put on their Sunday best and, suitcase in hand, took the trackless to Rotherham, then walked to Nellie's house. She was waiting for them and opened her door with a dramatic sweeping gesture. "Do come in! Make yourselves at home!"

William had barely laid down the overnight bag when Nellie began announcing plans for their visit. "Harry, you're to sleep down here on the settee. Look there, pet, I've placed a nice eiderdown there for you and a plump pillow. Edna and William, your bed in the guest room upstairs is all ready for you to have a nice, sound sleep tonight. If the air raid sirens go off, we can all head out to the shelter in the garden out back. There's room for the five of us!"

It being a fine day, Nellie had set up for tea outside: Delicate china cups and plates in a rose pattern, an elegantly-shaped matching china tea pot, and, 'though Edna didn't ask how and where she got them in the midst of rationing, a large plate filled with cucumber and chicken tea sandwiches and yet another with scones, iced cakes, clotted cream, and strawberry jam. Harry's eyes all but popped out of his head at the sight. His stomach began to rumble. The day was indeed fine and the two sisters, their husbands, and Harry enjoyed themselves in the garden. Harry savored every morsel.

Once the sun began to set and the air to cool, everyone went inside. A fire blazed in the lounge. Nellie set Harry to the task of closing all the blackout curtains, then left him to admire a collection of his aunt's and uncle's clocks while the grownups talked about the war, gossiped, and generally set the world to rights.

At last Nellie announced it was bedtime, words that were music to her guests' ears. Edna and William were exhausted, and Harry was looking forward to a good night's sleep under the soft eiderdown Auntie Nellie had set out for him. Soon everyone was in their respective places for sleep, all hoping that the night would be siren free. And it was.

But it turned out to be a terrible night's sleep for Harry, Edna, and William when they realized that Auntie Nellie and Uncle Harry's collection of at least 75 clocks placed throughout the house clanged, chimed, and cuckooed all night long—grandfather clocks, wall clocks, mantel clocks, Westminster chimes, Whittington chimes, St. Michael chimes, St. Clements chimes, and Winchester chimes, among others--each striking on their own top of the hour, quarter-hour, half-hour, and three-quarters-of-an-hour timeframes. Some sounded in sing-song unison, others in dissonance from each other as their pendulums swung and their independent mechanisms ticked, tocked, and whirred. At least eight different cuckoo clocks made a low dong-then high cuckoo at high pitches at different times within minutes of each other as the little mechanized birds popped in and out of the little doors of the little their little Black Forest houses. One silver-faced clock had delicate little tinkle bells. Harry tried to cut out the noise by pulling the eiderdown over his head—but it was of little use. His aunt and uncle had long since tuned out the racket and didn't notice the cacophony, but it was impossible for Harry, William, and Edna to do so.

When morning came, the three were truly the worse for wear. It was hard to believe that a night at Auntie Nellie's house could be as bad as—or worse—than a night in the Anderson shelter at home. But it was.

255

Nellie had prepared an abundant breakfast, once again with food that was hard to come by: She laid on eggs, kippers, bacon, stewed tomatoes, and toast with butter and marmalade. Edna, William, and Harry should have been thrilled—but they could scarcely keep their eyes open.

"What's the matter, you three?" asked Nellie. "You look like you didn't sleep a wink last night!"

Without saying a word, the three exhausted Baileys took one look at each other, then silently ate their breakfast.

The trip home to Rawmarsh was a tiring end to an exhausting visit to Doncaster Place. They approached 21 Moxon's Yard with relief, then William, Edna, and Harry retired to bed as quickly as they could after William lit the fire to re-heat the house.

The toll of war in this case was not from the sirens warning of potential air raids, but from the non-stop tolling overnight of Auntie Nellie's many clocks.

A Bomb Strikes Uncle Joe's Tram

(December 1940

Christmas was in the air—albeit a war-time Christmas without the usual trimmings—but one in which Harry looked forward to choir practice and the chance to delve into the music of the season. It took his mind off of the growing lack in every family's lives—less food, restrictions on clothing purchases, less fuel—and long, tedious queues in the cold for just about everything. Edna was gladder than she wanted to admit when Harry missed school due to air raid warnings. It meant he could share in the queuing for everything from soap to sausage.

And it took everyone's' minds off the horrifying November Coventry Blitz, which, among its tragedies, caused extensive damage not only to strategically important metal industries there, but also the city center and its beautiful medieval cathedral. Coventry was a mere 68 miles by air from the West Riding—a quick distance to cover in a bomber.

257

Harry was nervously excited about the arrival of Christmas. He had been given the honor of singing the opening verse of *Once, In Royal David's City*—his favorite carol—for the festival of lessons and carols at church. Just a few years previously before his voice broke Horace had sung the solo. Harry felt proud to now be following in his friend and mentor's footsteps.

It was a clear night with a beautiful full moon on 12 December. Harry had returned home from choir practice and was drawing by candlelight in his room on a bit of cardboard he had found. It was cold and he could see the condensation of his breath in the candlelight as it hit the chilly air. He wrapped himself up in a blanket and had his socks on to keep his feet warm. William was heating water for hot water bottles downstairs. It was just after 7:00 p.m. as Harry began to think about preparing to put on his pajamas. But that involved taking off his warm jumper and exposing his body to the cold air. Just as he decided to go ahead and change, the air raid siren, with its initial low moan that quickly rose to a higher pitch and steadily rising-falling-rising-falling tone, blared its warning across every street, hill, and valley. Monitoring stations had picked up the *X Verfahren* radio beams the

Luftwaffe bomber crews used as pathfinders to their target as they headed across the channel from northern France. On this cold and moonlit night, all indications were that Sheffield and its steel works and armaments factories would be attacked.

As the sirens blared, Edna, William, and Harry grabbed their coats and gas masks and scrambled to the Anderson Shelter. Nanan and Leonard were next—with William and Harry helping 64-year-old Nanan in as she found it difficult to crouch down to enter through the steel panel barrier at the entrance. The Coopers were only moments behind them. The families shivered both from the damp chill in the air and from fear. Fortunately, Edna had grabbed the hot water bottles from the kitchen table on the way out. She handed one to Harry to warm up and pass to Derek and Alan—and gave the other to Nanan.

Everyone knew what had happened to London, Coventry, Liverpool, Leeds, Manchester, and Bradford. The Nazis might fly over and attack those cities again—or this could be the attack on Sheffield, Rotherham, and the Parkgate Iron & Steelworks that everyone dreaded and assumed was inevitable.

The Luftwaffe began the long-anticipated bombing of Sheffield just 12 miles to the Southwest of Rawmarsh at 7:41 p.m. The distinctive drone of the German aircraft roared in the distance. The deafening sound of aircraft and anti-aircraft guns made it impossible to ignore what was happening outside the Anderson Shelter; sound carried easily through its corrugated steel shell. Everyone sat close and quietly. At other moments, they shuddered at the sound of aeroplanes not too far away.

Had it been safe for the Baileys to stand atop Rawmarsh Hill and look toward Sheffield, they would have seen a ghastly site. The clear sky over the city had turned a shocking yellow-orange from the fires engulfing parts of the city as the enemy bombarded it mercilessly, unleashing thousands of tons of high-explosive bombs that set massive fires, the flames and smoke of which spread rapidly. The flames were visible for miles.

But in the confines of the small Anderson Shelter at the back of Moxon's Yard all they could hear was the roar of aircraft and anti-aircraft guns reverberating across hill and dale. It was terrifying and relentless. The assault lasted for nine hours after the first warning sirens sounded. The final bombs to be dropped on Sheffield were at 4 a.m. on 13 December.

The dropping pitch of the air raid siren's all clear sound led to many thousands of households in the many villages and towns around Sheffield sighing in relief, with others enveloped in grief. Everyone was desperate for news of whether loved ones, friends, co-workers, and workplace had survived. In Sheffield itself, the sounds of the fire brigade's sirens and St. John's Ambulance lasted for hours more as the injured and dead were brought out of the bombed remains of homes and streets.

By morning word was out on the terrible destruction Sheffield endured. The cathedral was struck, a direct hit devastated the city's Marples Hotel, killing many with many more unaccounted for. Thousands of houses and businesses went up in flames, and passengers on trams and buses fled their transport all along the lines between Sheffield, Rotherham, Parkgate, and Rawmarsh. There was massive loss of life—and thousands became homeless overnight. Anyone and everyone were targets. And everyone knew they hadn't seen the last of the Luftwaffe.

On the night of the 15th, the air-raid sirens sounded as the Luftwaffe returned to attack Sheffield yet again. On this second attack, just two days after the first, Germany introduced a new method of attack. It set about to destroy its targets combining incendiaries that started fires, followed by high-explosive bombs that left huge craters in roads, making access for emergency crews extremely difficult, giving the fire more time to spread and destroy. In the first 50-minute wave of the attack, German pathfinders unleashed the payloads of sixteen Junkers 111s, which dropped fifteen incendiaries that set off fires large enough that they could be seen from over ninety miles away. In the next two-hour wave, fifty Heinkel 111s and eleven Dornier 17s dropped high-explosive bombs, hitting industrial targets including Steel, Peech & Tozer—where William and Uncle Harold worked—and Hadfields, Brown Bayleys Steelworks. Incredibly, in the midst of the terrible destruction, the damage to the steelworks was limited.

On the morning of 16 December, Auntie Elsie and Uncle Joe rode up to Moxon's Yard on his motorbike to check in on everyone. They wanted to be sure that everyone in Rawmarsh was well. Harry noticed immediately that Uncle Joe's usually energetic gait was far more measured—and he looked exhausted. "Uncle Joe, Are you all right?" Harry asked anxiously as they approached. Edna and Elsie gave each other a good long hug, each being a much-needed sisterly comfort to the other.

Uncle Joe then began to tell the tale of the night before: "I was on my tram shift, driving between Sheffield and Rotherham. It was dark as pitch. We were passing by the steelworks, when the air-raid sirens sounded. I stopped the tram and we all made a run for it to the public air raid shelter—men, women, and even a few tykes. I barely got my passengers to safety when everything began to shake and rumble. The roar of the bombers and the sounds of bombs exploding was awful beyond words. We spent a good four hours in the shelter before the all-clear. I wasn't sure if anything would be left standing. When we came out, all that was left of my tram was a burned-out hulk completely gutted by fire but for its frame. It was downright eerie, ghastly. If ever anything looked like the gates of Hell, then Sheffield did last night. There were smoke and rubble everywhere. We would have been dead for sure if we hadn't made it to that shelter. We all walked to Rotherham together with the stench of burning and the glow of the fires behind us. One poor lass was with child, so we took turns helping her along. There were buildings in flames behind us. It's the worst thing I've ever seen—so much destruction." He then looked away to compose himself before looking back. He continued, "So much brutality and loss of life."

Harry stared at him in shock and fascination. Noticing, Uncle Joe said, "Come 'ere lad," and extended open arms to his nephew to give him a hug, then looking straight into Harry's eyes he continued, "We will fight, and we will fight rather than let Hitler take us over. You can count on that, young Harry. You're not going to grow up under the wickedness of that monster." Harry's admiration for his uncle grew stronger than ever.

Just ten days before Christmas, huge areas of Sheffield's city center were in ruins. Fires smoldered for days. Well over 600 children, women, and men were counted as dead, over 1500 were injured, and over 40,000 were homeless. Several thousand homes were so badly damaged that they would need to be demolished. Thousands more houses had also been damaged in the two attacks.

But the people were unbroken. They committed themselves to getting on with things—and Christmas was Christmas not only in the best of times, but, perhaps more importantly, in the worst. Everyone did what they could to find a way to enjoy the beauty and of the holiday—and take strength from it. They weren't going to let Hitler destroy that, too.

Saint Mary's was full for the Christmas Eve choral service of lessons and carols. Harry was ready for his solo, despite a day full of butterflies in his stomach anticipating this moment. Each time he thought of how nervous he was, he thought of how brave Uncle Joe had been just days before—and it helped him calm his nerves.

As the service began, he stood at the front of the choir, his face glowing in candlelight, at the back of the narthex. Mr. Blyth, the organist and choirmaster, gave him his one-note cue to sing his solo *a capella*. Harry breathed in deeply, then, following the gentle prompting of the choir master, he began his solo in a clear, steady, soprano voice:

Once in royal David's city
stood a lowly cattle shed,
where a mother laid her baby
in a manger for his bed:
Mary was that mother mild,
Jesus Christ, her little child.

No one at the service was left unmoved by the clarity and beauty of Harry's voice. Some dabbed tears from their eyes. His voice and pitch had been unwavering as the organ and the full choir joined him in singing the second stanza and processed behind the cross toward the altar in the gentle glow of candlelight:

He came down to earth from heaven
who is God and Lord of all;
and his shelter was a stable,
and his cradle was a stall:
with the poor, and meek, and lowly
lived on earth our Savior holy.

At the transept, the choir turned to face the congregation, and all joined in singing:

Jesus is our childhood's pattern,
day by day like us he grew;

he was little, weak, and helpless,
tears and smiles like us he knew:
and he feels for all our sadness,
and he shares in all our gladness.
And our eyes at last shall see him,
through his own redeeming love,
for that child, so dear and gentle,
is our Lord in heaven above:
and he leads his children on
to the place where he has gone.
Not in that poor lowly stable
with the oxen standing by
we shall see him, but in heaven,
set at God's right hand on high;
there his children gather round,
bright like stars, with glory crowned.
--Cecil Frances Alexander

The deeply comforting sound of the many voices joined together in song was in sharp contrast to the frightful sounds of the recent nights of bombings. Those present experienced a collective and deep sense of all that was precious in their lives—something of the peaceful and sacred. For that time, they were able to stay present in the beauty of the moment, to briefly put aside their cares and longing to see their loved ones far from home fighting the war.

Harry, surrounded by his choir friends, felt a profound sense of comfort and joy as all the voices swelled together for the carol's closing words "...*there his children gather round, bright like stars, with glory crowned.*"

Cricket, Pancakes, and Peace

1942

It's a true Yorkshire expression: "*If you want to get your own way, take home your cricket bat.*" That's precisely what Harry did on a summer's afternoon after a heated disagreement with Derek, Alan, and a few other neighboring boys over whether or not he was *run out* playing cricket in the field behind the Regal. Harry took his cricket bat and stormed off home. It would have been one thing if the other boys had other bats at the ready to continue play—but in families with so few resources to go around, Harry was the only boy who owned a bat—and it was shared among the boys as a precious commodity. By asserting his rights of ownership and huffing off with the key instrument of play, he brought the game to an abrupt halt. Derek pleaded with Harry to come back and keep playing at first, then hurled the ball at the wickets in frustration, sending the stumps flying.

Marching resolutely, bat firmly in hand, Harry continued to storm his way home, threw open the door, and slammed it hard to shut it again, striding to the back kitchen. A weary-looking Edna, who had spent most of her day queuing with the family ration books for food and a few small bars of soap, was at the table preparing the family's tea, stretching their meager rations as far as she could. She had a small amount of flour and powdered eggs on hand, which she planned to set aside to make a Yorkshire Pudding on Sunday. There would be a little meat to accompany it if Mr. Downs had any she could afford. But it had been many months since the family had enjoyed a good Yorkshire pudding. She had determined to get one on the table this time, even a small one. She reasoned it would be good for family morale.

Harry avoided eye contact with Edna and was red in the face as he entered the kitchen. She surveyed his increasingly lanky, thin frame. Harry rested his bat against the table and didn't bother to pick it up when it fell over with a clatter onto the linoleum. He dropped into a chair at the table in a sulk. At first Edna let him have his sulk as she turned her attention to turning up the low flame on the cooker, trying to get more heat for cooking. Then, after a few minutes of Harry's silence and tap-tap-tapping on the floor restlessly with his foot, she drew him out to find out what had brought on such a cloudy and usually-out-of-character demeanor.

When he finally began to talk, she listened to how he and the neighboring boys had their falling out. She heard his anger and frustration—then noted that he had left the other boys without the one bat they all used to play their games.

"Come 'ere, Lad," she said softly to Harry, "You and Derek and Alan are pals. We don't need you boys fighting one another when Hitler's bombs are being dropped on us and so many more people around the world, maiming and killing men, women, and children. You boys need to get along and be good to each other."

Harry folded his long, thin arms onto the table and dropped his head onto the table in a further gesture of sulkiness. His bony elbows pointed out. Edna, undaunted by his efforts to block her out, continued: "And thou's the only boy on t' yard with a bat. With so little to go around between us all, we need to take good care of our neighbours and share what we have as best we can with one another. If tha goes and takes t' one cricket bat, t' other boys can't go on with t'play.

No fight over a game is worth hurting our friendship and peace with t'other boys."

He thought quietly about his mother's words for a minute or so. He wanted to be in the right, to go on being mad at the other boys, but he could no longer remember what set him off in the first place. It was only a game after all.

Harry's shoulder blades heaved through the thinning cloth of this shirt as he breathed heavily in and out. Finally, he raised his head slowly and looked over at the family's gas masks hanging from hooks on the back wall. He looked at the bat, now lying on the red linoleum without purpose or play. After another heave of his thin shoulders he conceded quietly to Edna, "Aye, mother."

And as he looked up at her he saw that she had pulled out the family's small supply of flour and powdered eggs. She began measuring some of each into a mixing bowl. She then added powdered milk, water, a pinch of salt, baking powder, and the little sugar she had on hand. She touched Harry gently on the elbow. "Come then, we are going to make pancakes for you and your mates. There may be no peace in the big world beyond, but we will have it here among neighbours and friends on Moxon's Yard."

Harry's thin face brightened. He began mixing the thick, ivory-coloured batter. Edna heated a cast iron frying pan on a ring on the cooker, then, satisfied that it was hot enough, added a small knob of butter to the pan and swirled it around to cover as much of the pan's surface as she could. She began ladling out batter that sizzled as it hit the hot surface. Soon the kitchen filled with the scent of cooking pancakes—a scent that had long been absent from the house. Harry inhaled the steam with longing and joy. Edna and Harry took turns pouring and tending the batter, then transferring the thin pancakes to a plate. When the pancakes were cool enough to touch, mother and son folded them into halves, then into triangular-shaped cakes. Edna took a teaspoon of their remaining precious sugar supply and sprinkled it over the warm, golden-edge treats.

"Right then lad," said Edna gently but firmly, "It's time to make peace with your friends." Harry's face clouded over for an instant, then, with a shy smile he picked up his bat. Edna picked up the plate of pancakes. The two headed to the front door and out into Moxon's Yard.

The other boys were leaning against the wall of the Regal across from the houses, scowls on their faces. They focused their eyes elsewhere in a posture of studied indifference as Harry emerged from the house. But then, when they saw Edna coming out behind Harry with a plate in her hands, their curiosity overcame them.

Harry and Edna walked over to the boys. Their eyes widened with delight at the sight of the pancake treats. They quickly gathered around Edna and Harry.

Edna spoke up first. "Here then, lads. We are all to be friends. Thous not to fight with one another. We need each other and to live in peace as good friends and neighbours." The boys all stared down at their feet in a mix of embarrassment and sheepish acceptance of Edna's words. Sensing they were in need of relief from their feelings, Edna chimed, "Go on, then. Each have some pancakes and all 'us be friends."

The boys looked up with smiles on their faces and brightness in their eyes. They looked each other in the eye and then, giggling one after another, made their peace with each other. They each then helped themselves to one of the thin, warm, sweet pancakes from the plate Edna held out in offering to them.

"Ta, Mother Bailey," Derek said, and then they all said "Ta" in turn to Edna—accepting her kindness and counsel. They then bit into the treats. The soft, warm pancakes spread a hint of sweetness across their mouths. It had been a long time since they had enjoyed such a treat. It was bliss.

After each having a second pancake each, they thanked Edna again and were ready to go back to their game. "Let's go have a knock, then," said Harry cheerfully. The other boys nodded their heads in agreement, and they all headed back to the field behind the Regal. Harry's bat was quickly returned to play. As Edna heard the sounds of laughter and the ball hitting the bat she smiled, then returned inside with the empty plate.

Peace has been accomplished with the help of Edna's precious rations and the wisdom of a mother who knew that games were not worth fighting over and that the lesson in friendship was worth the sacrifice of rations her family had just made.

A Business Concern: Mr. Willey the Butcher

1943

"Young Harry, come here lad!" said Mr. Willey, the local butcher whose shop was on High Street just past The Regal. He had known Harry since he was a small boy—and now, seeing Harry looking so thin for a growing young man, he was worried about him. He had something in mind: He needed help with the pigs he raised in the small green space behind his shop—and had always entrusted the job over the years to a Moxon's Yard child he trusted to do a good job.

"Hello, sir," said Harry, surprised by the sudden burst of attention by the usually busy butcher.

"Look here, lad, I've got a problem. I'm so busy in t'shop and managing the ration coupons that I have no time t' feed and fuss with my pigs out back. There's none of us who has time, not a one. So...I got to thinking you might be able to help. I've seen you scratching the pigs' ears and speaking nicely to them on your way to and from school. You're a fine lad to be trusted. Would you help me with the feeding of them?"

Harry looked interested, so the butcher continued: "You go up and down Moxon's Yard and collect what's in the pig swill bins—all the peelings and left-overs—and bring it all to my shop. I'll show you how to help me boil it up with pig meal in the copper, then feed the pigs. As pay, I'll give you a pound of our fresh pork sausage—about four links—each weekend. That will be something nice you can bring home to your mum and dad for your supper. And at Christmas I'll send as nice a juicy joint as I can to your mum."

Harry was astonished—pleasantly so. A sausage a week each for Harry, Edna, and William was something money couldn't buy with rationing.

"Mr. Willey, that would be grand!" Harry said happily, then paused, "Is it all right? Er...I mean I know it's not on the ration."

"Go on lad," said Mr. Willey with a hearty, kindly laugh. "It's your *pay*. You'll be helping me out—and trust me, lad, the pigs like you more than they like me!"

Harry smiled and laughed, and without another moment's thought on the proposition said, "Well then yes, Mr. Willey, I'd be happy to do it and my mum and dad will be ever so pleased."

"Good lad. Then we'll start in the morning, say 8:00 before you go to school. I'll show you where everything is that you need—and before you know it the pigs will be pointing their snouts toward your direction and waiting at the fence for you each morning. They'll like you even more than they already do!"

"Yes, Mr. Willey, I'll come 'round in the morning before school. Thank you!" With that Mr. Willey extended his right hand toward Harry's and the two shook hands on the arrangement. Harry then headed toward home, smiling and standing taller and walking with more energy. He looked forward to telling Edna and William and Nanan about his new job. Mr. Willey stood on the sidewalk and watched him go, chuckled, then returned into his shop. He did need Harry's help—and he was glad to be able to help him in the bargain.

And for the remaining weeks, then months, then years ahead throughout the war, Harry fed the pigs every morning and collected potato peels and other kitchen scraps from bins behind each of the neighbors' houses. As agreed, once a week Mr. Willey sent him home with a parcel of plump sausages. Harry felt proud each time when he handed it over to Edna. They tasted even better than ever.

Edna tried to thank Mr. Willey once early on in the arrangement. The sausages were a godsend. "Oh, Mrs. Bailey, your Harry is the one to thank. He's a cracking fine lad and the pigs love him. He doesn't just feed them as I asked. He's truly kind to them. He fusses over them, talks to them, scratches their ears. He's compassionate. I am the one to be thanking *you* for raising such a fine lad. I'm right chuffed with our arrangement." Edna smiled, the cares vanishing briefly from her care-worn face, "Well he's a good son and he thinks the world of you, Mr. Willey. Let me thank you for that then."

"Ah, good enough Mrs. Bailey! Just know I think the world of your Harry and I'm glad that he's happy with our arrangement." Just then the bell rang on the shop's front door as another customer stepped in, ration book in hand. Mr. Willey gave Edna a friendly wink, then greeted his new customer. Edna smiled, hitched her wicker market basket higher up her arm, said good day, then headed home.

"See you next time Mrs. Bailey, said Mr. Willey. "You were kind to drop by."

Harry had helped Mr. Willey as he ran his busy business— and Mr. Willey had found a way to help a poor child not only eat a bit better, but also feel valued.

Back Down the Pit

1943

With the war in full swing across Europe and North Africa, production at Steele, Peech and Tozer—or "Steelo's"—was in full swing day and night. William had now worked there with full employment for three years, working his way up and making a bit more each time. There would be many more days and years of work there ahead as new steel came off the rolling mills and open-hearth furnaces glowed day and night to melt scrap steel for munitions, from gun barrels to armor plate to support the Allied effort.

Around the clock the works were a loud, hot inferno with glowing furnaces and flying sparks. Before the war, when the shops were full of goods, the Baileys and so many other working families could not afford what was then so readily available. Now, finally, William brought home enough with his wages there that the family could afford a bit more—but now there were rations on purchases of everything including food, clothing, and other essential items like soap.

William worked with his brother-in-law Harold and many of his mates from Rawmarsh in conditions far less dangerous than the mines. It was a step up after decades of working in the mines. Even as the steelworks were a prime target for the Luftwaffe, he was glad to be above ground making better money in a safer job. Edna was glad, too. There was more money coming into the house and less coal dust coming into the house and making its way in and settling on every surface. Most of all, the gnawing anxiety that William wouldn't come home alive from a pit accident had been her constant and unwelcome companion, a fear that was a longstanding part of the very fabric of community life.

But now, in 1943, the government had a serious problem: Early in the war it had made the mistake of calling up too many miners for the armed services and war effort—so there weren't enough miners now to mine the ever-growing amount of coal needed to fuel the war effort. The shortage of miners meant reduced production. Without coal the very fight to win the war was at stake. The coal supply was becoming perilously low and desperately needed to fuel key manufacturing and transportation. Something had to be done—and quickly.

The government made an appeal to all able-bodied former miners not in the armed services to return to the pit—to include an increase in their rations to sustain their labour. The government had made a promise that anyone who returned to the mines could return to the steelworks with a guaranteed job on their return. William felt that he had no choice but to do his duty and return if what was at stake was his family's and the nation's future. Edna tried to talk him out of it, and some of his friends at the pub ignored it and told William to ignore the call and not be so "daft" as to return underground. But other friends decided, like him, to do what the government asked for. The promise that he could get his job back in the steelworks after the war was won was good enough assurance for William, so, following procedure, he informed the management at Steel, Peech & Tozer and braced himself for a return to the physically demanding, dangerous work of a miner. He was now 42 years old. It would be far more difficult to move around and crouch in narrow spaces underground now than even a few years before.

Harry heard William rise early and go downstairs on his first day returning to the mine. He got out of bed and followed him downstairs. Harry was filled with a mix of sadness and pride in his dad as he saw him organize his snap tin and cold tea to bring down the pit with him. William took one look at Harry and said without hesitation, "Tha's not going down 't' pit if I can help it, Harry. Your studies are what matter most. We don't need two daft buggers carrying a shovel for a living in this family."

Harry's eyes rose up solemnly and met his dad's. He slowly and quietly nodded his understanding and agreement with him. William continued, "The reason I am going back down the pit is because of you, Elsie, Audrey, Irene, Dorothy, Ernest, Jack, and Dennis. You children deserve a better future."

Harry stepped closer to William, nodded his understanding, and hugged his dad. William gulped to hold in his tears. He didn't want Harry to see him cry. After a few moments, he gave Harry and extra squeeze, then collected his gear, said good-bye, and headed out the door to work.

Despite the government's appeal, there was still a shortage of miners, so, desperate for a solution, young men enlisted or enlisting in the armed forces were instead sent to work down the mines, to be chosen through a lottery no enlisted man wanted to be selected for. The result was over 48,000 raw recruits were transported to mines in the West Riding and around the country—ten percent of all military recruits between ages 18-25. These young men thought they would be fighting in Europe or somewhere else overseas, perhaps in India or the Far East, but were instead transported to mines in England and Wales to work in the pits alongside the experienced miners. The recruit miners were nicknamed Bevin Boys after the former trade unionist and Labour politician who was serving as Minister of Labour and National Service in the coalition government. Some Bevin Boys, a small minority, were also known as *optees* for volunteering to work in the mines rather than go overseas.

These young recruits were in for a shock. Many had never seen the harsh human landscape and conditions of the industrial north—and knew nothing of the difficult conditions and gruelling physical work underground. It was enormously traumatic to them—the claustrophobia, heat, cold, wet—and the back-breaking work. Further, most were billeted with local families, and not always particularly welcome in homes that were already too small for the number of inhabitants.

For experienced miners like William, the idea of working alongside so many inexperienced miners in dangerous conditions alarmed him, but he did his best to show them the ropes. Some were only a few years older than Harry. They all deserved better. And that belief is what sustained William each day as he mined coal once again.

Off to Mexborough

September 1944

After the trauma of failing the eleven-plus exam at nine and finally being able to re-take it at Haugh Road two years later at eleven, Harry had passed the exam and gained entrance to Mexborough Grammar School. William, Edna, and all the family were elated and incredibly proud of Harry. The only catch was that three years later he was still waiting for a place to open. The financial sacrifice to the family would be enormous, but both William and Edna were determined that Harry deserved the chance they never had as children to continue school and fulfill his potential.

Horace Bailey blazed the trail: He defied the odds and lit the way for Harry when he enrolled at Mexborough, still determined to study medicine. Given his lowly station in life, his dream had seemed an outlandish one to others, as seemingly unlikely as saying he would one day fly to the moon. But his dream made perfect sense to him. Holding steadfastly to it fuelled a sense of possibility in him that little else in the circumstances of his life reinforced.

Nothing could lessen Horace's determination to become a doctor, despite even well-intentioned Mexborough teachers sometimes counseling him to lower his sights because he lacked both money and social standing to study medicine. Still, with personal determination and the support of mentors at a series of sometimes small, sometimes key but always pivotal moments, Horace did the seemingly impossible: He passed his A-Level exams at Mexborough with flying colours and gained acceptance into medical school at University of Sheffield. It was the fulfillment of the goal of becoming a doctor he had set for himself as a bereft child after his father's death.

Now, in August 1944, a major shift in national policy created a new opportunity for Harry, too. After input from all parties in the government, Education Secretary R.A. Butler shepherded the Education Act of 1944 through Parliament. It was the beginning of a massive re-structuring of education in the nation—and one practical benefit was that Harry's educational opportunities broadened. The number of children advancing to higher education at fourteen would now triple from 1% of students to 3%—still a micro-minority of students—but one of which Harry was now to be a part. There would be a few more working-class students at Mexborough, Harry would be one of them. It was a chance.

As the sun rose on the September morning of the first day at Mexborough, an acrid, opaque smog hung over Moxon's Yard, Rawmarsh Hill, and the valley, just like countless others before that had hung like a black veil. It was to be Harry's first day as a student at Mexbrough School. With the summer school holiday over, Harry's childhood was further transmuting into a new season of young adulthood. He awoke feeling both queasy and strangely energized after a fitful night's sleep.

He rose and got out of bed, thinking "That's it then. It's time to get a move on." He swung his feet out from under the covers and onto the peg rug beside his bed before stepping onto the cool red lino floor. He splashed his face with water from the bowl and pitcher, then dried it off and parted the blackout curtains to look out the window across the middens to the barely visible rooftops and smoking chimneys on Pottery Street. He heard Edna downstairs rattling about in the kitchen fixing his breakfast and heating water to start the Monday morning laundering. Harry's attention returned to the window as he studied his reflection on the glass. He had been anticipating this day all summer, sometimes with eager anticipation and other times with dread. Was he up to it? Clever enough? The ordeal of his failed eleven-plus exam still had the power to haunt him even though five years had passed since he took it and failed at nine. Would he fit in at Mexborough? Horace had now left for medical school. He wouldn't be there to ride the trackless with Harry or offer a watchful, protective eye as he had done for so many years. It was all new. For the first time in his life, Harry's school wasn't a short walk up the street with children he knew. It wasn't even in Rawmarsh. He knew none of the teachers, He'd even be having his school lunches there instead of coming home for lunch. It was in turns nerve-wracking and exciting.

Dressing for school was different, too. He looked across his dim-lit room at a deep green Mexborough school blazer with school crest stitched on its front pocket. The blazer was new to him, but not new. It was a bit worn in places, especially the elbows, where its previous wearer must have leaned frequently. It was a bit too wide for his thin frame—and a bit short at the sleeves for his long limbs. It had made its way to him through Nanan and a member of the Mother's Union at St. Mary's. Had it not been for this, he'd be wearing his regular, increasingly threadbare clothes.

The rationing of clothes had begun in 1941—with each adult entitled to 66 coupons per year at the start—and growing children allowed an extra 10 points. Point value was assigned to every garment, so that money alone did not dictate who could and could not buy clothes. As the war progressed the number of coupons per person fell as the government did its best to ensure some kind of equitable distribution with increasingly limited resources. Everyone did their best to stretch the life out of their garments by mending, bartering, and doing without some items. Each clothing purchase involved a trade-off of some sort.

Clothes prices had risen over the course of the first years of the war. Edna had saved money and ration coupons for months to buy Harry two new white dress shirts. They now hung next to his blazer on a peg in his room, freshly washed and crisply ironed for this first day at his new school. Edna vowed to do all she could to make sure that Harry was able to meet the school's uniform rules, which had relaxed little despite the war. And on Harry's desk, his new green Mexborough cap—each student was required to wear one—rested archly next to a Mexborough tie Horace had passed on to him. His black canvas plimsolls lay in wait on the floor, stuffed with a pair of black socks Edna had darned yet again to extend their life. A new pair of dark trousers was folded over the back of his chair, a gift made possible by all his aunts and uncles pooling ration coupons. And even the ever-critical Grandfather Dyson, proud of his grandson without saying so in words, arrived on the Sunday a week before school started to present Harry with a brown leather school satchel for his books. At his grandfather's insistence, on the spot Harry carefully wrote his name and address on the small white paper name card that fit into a pocket at its front.

Harry dressed himself. The new trousers were somewhat itchy on his legs and were roomy so that he could grow into them. He was proud to be wearing trousers instead of the shorts of boyhood. His dress shirt was roomy, too, a size too big, so he could grow into it. He put on his tie and blazer, then caught a glimpse of his reflection in the windowpane: Too loose collar aside, he was beginning to look the part of a real Mexborough student. He slipped on his socks and plimsolls, picked up his satchel, grabbed his cap, and made his way downstairs.

"Ooh, you do look a real scholar!" cooed Edna with pride as she placed a bowl of porridge down for him and poured a cup of weak tea from re-used tea leaves for Harry. They were close to the end of their sugar ration, but she sprinkled a bit into the porridge and tea to honour the special day.

Nervous about the day ahead, Harry poked at the porridge with his spoon. "Mum, I'm just not hungry right now. My stomach is all topsy-turvy."

"Have some tea, at least," Edna replied, "You've got a full day ahead of you and who knows when you'll have your school dinner. At least you will have free school meals. That's a godsend."

Harry took a few sips of tea to assuage Edna's motherly fussing, then rose abruptly from the table with a strong sense of urgency. "I've got to go now, mum. I can't miss the trackless or I'll be in for it."

"Right then, son," Edna replied. She reached for her cardigan. "Let's go." Harry grabbed the cardboard box holding his goggle-eyed gas mask and positioned the strap to his satchel on his shoulder. The two headed out.

Mary Ellen Cooper was already outside polishing her front step and lining it with donkey stone. War or no war, standards needed to be maintained. "Aye-yo then Harry," she chirped, 'Enjoy your first day! You do look smart. My boys will look forward to seeing you at supper time."

"Thank you, Mrs. Cooper," Harry replied before he and Edna continued walking quickly toward High Street. They took a right to pass by the Regal toward the trackless stop across from the Methodist Church. Mr. Willey was already in his shop laying out sausages in the glass case and tapped on the window and waved at Harry and Edna as they hurried by. Harry and Edna looked down High Street toward St. Mary's to catch a glimpse of the tram headlights, still partially covered with black on the top half to make it difficult to see from the air.

Two other older Mexborough students were already standing at the stop. Harry quickly noticed that their uniforms were newer and fit them better—and they both wore shiny, freshly polished black leather shoes, not canvas plimsolls like his. He wanted to hide his feet in that moment. While he was a student at Haugh Road School, he was like most of the other children he knew at school in Rawmarsh: Working class and poor. Now, despite his Mexborough blazer, tie, and cap, he stood out: His footwear was clearly inferior. He felt embarrassed.

Just then, Alfred Ward, one of the two students, a tall and lanky older boy he knew through Tommy Jacques and cricket, strode straight toward Harry and Edna in his Mexborough green school colors. He smiled and said, "Hey then, Harry! You're a Mexborough boy now." Sizing up Harry's worried look quickly, he added, "Don't worry if you feel a bit out of sorts at first. I certainly did on my first day. Come on then and we'll sit together on the trackless." He smiled broadly at Edna, then patted Harry on the back.

Just then Harry and Edna heard the buzzing, high-pitched vibrating sounds of an approaching tram. Next, emerging from the fog, a Mexborough & Swinton Traction Company Sunbeam trackless coach began to pierce through the smog heading from around the corner at the Earl Grey. It already had several people on it—mostly Mexborough students—when it stopped in front of them.

"Right then, son, you're ready for this," said Edna, standing back as the doors swung open. Harry nodded solemnly, then, following closely behind Alfred, he stepped up into the carriage and followed him to one of the open seats. The doors snapped shut. Harry peered out the window and briefly exchanged glances with Edna once again. She took a few more steps back, then turned to watch as the trackless pulled away. Harry couldn't see it, but she had tears in her eyes from her mixed feelings of pride for him and a sense of wistfulness as Harry began a new phase of life. Her little tyke was growing up quickly into a fine Yorkshireman and scholar.

"Look here, then, Harry!" said Alfred as the trackless whirred along. "As a sixth former I know my way around. If anyone gives you grief, they'll answer to me. We'll have none of their nonsense. Mexborough's a good place. You will get on just fine. Knowing you, I've no doubt you'll make friends and the teachers will like you. I think you'll like it. There's a world beyond Rawmarsh and the swimming baths after all, y' know." he chuckled, with a wink.

With that, Harry's face, which had been tense up 'til then, softened into a small, shy smile. His shoulders dropped as his tension fell and he relaxed his back a bit. The two boys then sat silently together enjoying the ride as the trackless wound and veered its way past one colliery, slag heap, foundry, or power plant after another through Swinton, then crossed over the Dearne River, picked up more students, then pulled into bustling Mexborough. Harry watched the comings and goings of munitions workers headed to or from work. He took in the too-frequently-empty shop windows, cinema marquees promoting films starring Margaret Rutherford and David Niven, the many billboards, and newsagents' sidewalk signs with headlines about the war written across them. As close as it was to Rawmarsh, the ride made Harry feel like a new, wider world was opening up. He thought, too, of the friends he left behind in Rawmarsh and wished he had the security of their being together with him. He'd miss seeing them every day.

"Sometimes this ride seems like a long haul, especially in the winter when it's dark," chirped Alfred. "You can always get some kip if you want, but the ride's never two days the same. Never. Mark my words: There's always something new to see. I make a game of it. One day it's what's new at the cinema in Swinton, the next it's watching birds fly in formation for the winter. Of course, you can always watch all the activity at the collieries." Harry nodded. The two fell back into friendly silence until the trackless stopped at College Road just down the street from the school. Alfred and Harry jostled off with all the other students in a sea of Mexborough green and headed up the road toward the handsome, imposing, Edwardian-era red-brick building.

"Here's the funny part," said Alfred as they approached the school, "Boys enter just here through the doors at this right side—look up—it even says 'BOYS.' And the lasses cross to the other side to enter at the left through the GIRLS side. But once inside we'll all mix in together! A bit daft really, but there it is!" He winked at Harry, who smiled. "Oh—and one more thing," continued Alfred, "Across the road there, that's the Cabbage Patch—I've seen more than a few bloody great enormous Henkels and Junkers fly overhead—godawful things—loud, too. It's a great place to watch our Lancaster bombers fly over. Magnificent! Oh, and on the subject, the air raid shelters are there, too, there next to the playing field. Ooh—and there's plenty of cricket at this school—war or no war!"

With that, Alfred, turned back toward the school. "Come on then Harry! Let's get you sorted!" And with that he escorted Harry into the building to the large assembly hall at its center. Harry looked up at the high ceilings and dark-beamed Arts & Crafts-style rafters, then around him. Students and some teachers were looking down into the hall from the open second floor corridors. Alfred tapped his elbow, then escorted him to a queue of new students being checked in by staff.

"Bailey, Harry...to the left. That's right. Next!"

Harry joined a group of other new students. His sense of unease rose again as he saw Alfred disappear to join the sixth form and saw so many smartly dressed students in well-fitted uniforms—all wearing leather shoes. He saw a few boys look at his feet, then whisper to each other, laugh, then turn away. The colour rose in Harry's cheeks.

Just then he noticed another new boy, one without any kind of uniform, just a plain white shirt, trousers, and a clip-on tie that was slightly too short. The other boy, gregarious by nature and perhaps sensing a kindred spirit, stepped up beside Harry and introduced himself: "Me name is Douglas Axe— but call me Larry for short—like Larry, Curly, and Moe like t' Three Stooges. What's your name then?"

Harry was a bit taken aback but liked this boy straight away. There was no pretense about him, just clear, intense raw intelligence. Before Harry spoke, Larry continued, "I don't know what to make of this place. Fanciest group of tykes I've ever seen except in posh films. Smart, too, mostly. That part I don't mind. I'm 'ere on scholarship. Smart enough I guess— and lucky. No brass for fancy togs like a green blazer and cap, but aye-oh, it's a chance, I'nt it?!" He looked intensely straight into Harry's eyes, then continued, "You from 'round here then?"

"Rawmarsh," replied Harry. "I'm here on scholarship, too," He added quietly with a small smile.

"Oh, Rawmarsh, I've been there once on the trackless! Well, more like through it. Nice parish church on the hill. We went to Rotherham once, me Mum and I. I'm keen on history and wanted to see the house on the bridge where they kept

Mary, Queen of Scots for one night on her way to being held for years at Hardwick Hall by t'Earl of Hardwick for our Good Queen Bess." Harry was silent, not sure he knew the story. "Do you not know the story, then?" Doug asked. "Aye, they kept the Scots queen locked in the place in Rotherham with the River Don running right underneath it. Don't know why, but Tudor history fascinates me. Henry VIII, Six Wives, Bloody Mary, the Virgin Queen, t'Spanish Armada. Funny that!"

The two boys fell silent, then watched in awe as Dr. Gwen Black, the headmistress, dressed in a smart tweed suit, strode to the front of the groups for the assembly as another teacher sat at a grand piano there. The students took seats by form, with Harry and Larry following the lead of others. With the sound of a bell all fell silent.

"Good morning students," said Dr. Black with authority, "Welcome to the new year and new term at Mexborough. Most of you know the school and what we expect of you— great things of which *you* are highly capable. To those of you who are new here today, we are glad that you are here. You will soon come to know what's expected—and what it means to be part of this great school where we value the life of the mind and encourage you to think of learning as your lifelong habit. So now…as we start a new year, let us first bow our heads and remember the Mexborough students who now, as we assemble, are off at war facing every kind of danger so that we may continue to learn in freedom. We give thanks to these fine men and women." The hall fell silent.

Harry and Larry did their best to take it all in—the impressive headmistress, the smart and serious-looking teachers, the older students, the green uniforms *en masse*. Some new students looked bewildered, while others who had been there a while were self-assured or putting on a good act of being so—and close to adulthood. It was daunting and thrilling all at once.

Soon the opening remarks ended, and within a moment the teacher at the piano struck the keys and students and teachers alike all sprang to their feet on cue to sing:

"God save our gracious king,
long live our noble king,
God save the king.
Send him victorious, happy and glorious,
long to reign over us.

God save the king."

The music teacher then transitioned to a new tune, the school song *Of Don and Dearne*:

> *"Far through ageless vaults of time*
> *Clear the sounds that call sublime*
> *The glad notes upward wing.*
> *Lore-strong spirits here are bred*
> *Whose worth outvies their sires,*
> *Talented greeted, achievement sped,*
> *In the proudest of the shires,*
> *Where the white rose blows*
> *And youth calls, by Don and Dearne."*
> *--F. Langley*

The assembly continued with announcements, then it was time to head to class. Harry and Larry followed their assigned teacher to the classroom. There would be a full schedule of English, maths, biology, geometry, physical education, and French to immerse in due time, but first, more placement exams to take.

As they passed by it, Harry noticed quickly that the large school library was full of books, encyclopedias, even gramophone records. He began to feel that, as Horace had assured him, he could fit in here. As daunting as it was, it was even more interesting and had far more to offer than the schools he had attended in Rawmarsh.

◆ ◆ ◆

After an exciting and exhausting first day and week of classes and trackless rides, one school day led to another. Harry fell into a rhythm of school and study, rising with enthusiasm most mornings, making a new friend or two on the trackless ride to school, and earning the respect of his teachers for his solid work and good thinking. He went about things quietly but was not a pushover. He became known and liked for his friendly, serious, gentle nature. Even some initial taunts at Harry, Larry, and other scholarship students soon gave way to respect for him. He may have worn plimsolls, was on free school dinners, and "working class," but his intelligence, character—and emerging height—made him a positive presence.

For his friend Larry, each week was more of a struggle. He was clearly intelligent, but he was struggling in some classes. He had done well in his previous school but now, surrounded by so many students who had better preparation and struggling against the weight of troubles at home, fuelled by the gnaw of poverty, he found it hard to find his footing. Some teachers were indifferent to his situation. His continuing lack of ability to afford the school uniform made him a constant target for cruel remarks from some students whose own self-worth depended on putting down others. Larry actually was doing better in some subjects than he had at his previous school, but overall, he was losing confidence.

Harry and Larry enjoyed each other's company. Harry enjoyed his friend's forthrightness and sense of humor. Larry appreciated that Harry had a sense of humor in his own way and knew that Harry understood him better than anyone else at school.

Harry got along well with most of the students, and especially appreciated the deep intelligence of another of the scholarship students, a local Mexborough boy named Ted Hughes, whose father, a former miner, owned a news and tobacco agent in town that they passed on the trackless on the way to school. Where Larry was forthright and more boisterous in spirit, Ted was quiet, intense, articulate, and interested in deep thinking. His sister Olwyn, two years older, was also at Mexborough. She shared her brother's quick intelligence. To Harry, her blonde hair and sense of self-assurance made her almost other-worldly. She was unlike any girls Harry knew in Rawmarsh.

Harry found and made friends at Mexborough, including some like Larry, who drew out his initial shyness, and others, like Ted, who inspired and shared his budding intellectual curiosity and interests. He would need to work hard at school, but he was glad of the chance to be a student there.

Auntie Nellie's Special Stew

1944

"Ooh, Harry, but you do look a skeleton!" said Auntie Nellie in her usual forthright, undiplomatic, yet well-intended way as she paid a visit to Edna on a Saturday afternoon and took one look at her nephew. "We've got to do something to get you fattened up. How's a lad to grow big, strong, and handsome on the rations we're getting?"

"Leave him be, Nellie," said Edna, who had been quietly worrying the same thing but not wanting to dwell on it. Everyone was doing their best to make the most of the food they had. They'd even become accustomed to the dried egg powder from America that had become a diet staple, getting beyond the initial horror at the idea of it to actually enjoying them scrambled.

"Auntie, I'm all right," said Harry in a not-convincing way. "I have as much food as any boy my age."

"Oh, but none look as skinny as you do! You don't have any fat on you!" replied Nellie, pinching Harry's rib cage and making him wriggle involuntarily. "Look, why don't you come for tea at my house Saturday next and I'll make something nice for you to put some fat on your bones! I'll make my special stew!"

Harry, a bit unsure, looked to Edna, who nodded her approval, then said, "That'll be grand!" knowing that Auntie Nellie always seemed to have something extra and special in her larder.

"Thank you. I will!" said Harry. The following week, Harry dressed up in his school dress shirt, tie, and cardigan. Even if the knit was increasingly frayed, he looked smart. He rode the trackless to Rotherham, then to Auntie Nellie's house there on Doncaster Place.

As he entered her house, he heard the infamous clocks by the dozens ticking, tocking, chiming, and clanging away at varying intervals. It reminded him of the sleepless night he'd had there with William and Edna four years earlier. He smiled to himself at the memory of that misadventure. He also picked up the mouthwatering scent of a wonderful meal.

"Ooh, Harry, you do look a handsome young man these days. We just need to fatten you up!" cooed Nellie as she led him into the house. Harry blushed.

"Come lad, I've made a lovely stew for you! Come and sit." Her movements were brisk with excitement. Harry's eyes lit up at the sight of her pretty dining table set with a lace tablecloth, delicate floral-motif china plates, and a crystal vase with fresh-cut flowers from her garden in it. Auntie Nellie made her way into the kitchen and returned, carrying a deep serving dish full to the brim with a hearty stew full of chunks of carrots, potatoes, peas, meat, and a thick gravy. She placed it at the center of the table. Its rich scent filled the air as steam illuminated by the sunlight streaming into the room rose from it.

Harry could barely contain his astonishment. He had not seen a stew like that since before the war began, and even back then, nothing ever as hearty as the stew before his eyes now.

"Don't stand there gawking, Harry!" Auntie Nellie said playfully. She was fond of her nephew. "Sit down right there and tuck in!"

Harry pulled out his chair, sat down, placed the carefully ironed serviette on his lap, and watched hungrily as Auntie Nellie set a plate of the hot, freshly ladled stew before him.

"There lad, enjoy this! You haven't seen a stew like this for quite some time, that I know!" said Nellie, beaming with pride at her kitchen creation.

Harry lowered his face to take in the scent rising with the steam. "Thank you, Auntie! It looks amazing and smells wonderful! Thank you!"

He marveled further as he asked, "How did you ever find this much meat at once?" in amazement at the sight and abundance before him.

"Best not to ask questions like that with a war on!" Nellie replied with a wink and a laugh. After serving herself, she sat down across from her nephew. She watched with pleasure as Harry tucked into her stew and a greatly satisfied expression took hold of and spread across his features.

"Do you like it, then?" asked Nellie, all but rhetorically.

"Aye, it's wonderful!" replied Harry happily before continuing to eat more.

As he was close to finishing what was on his plate, Harry said, "I haven't had beef for so long that I was wondering if I'd know what it would taste like!"

"Beef? Oh lad, that's not beef!" Nellie chuckled. She saw a quizzical expression form across Harry's face on this surprising news.

"Then if it's not beef, what is it?" asked Harry, as he looked at the remaining dark meat on his plate, now knowing that it wasn't what he thought it was.

"Horse, lad! It's horse meat!" said Nellie with pride at the fact that she had got her hands on some.

Harry all but dropped his fork on his plate. An expression of deep shock filled his face as he looked down at where his stew had been. "Horse? Oh auntie…I couldn't…I mean… had I known…*Horse*??" Harry was horrified. Had it come to this? Eating horse went against the grain, even if he was hungry. His appetite stalled. A pit formed in his stomach.

"Come now, Harry!" replied Nellie, surprised by the shock that had taken over her nephew. "Horse cooks up nicely! Don't let it go to waste now. There's plenty more—

and there's no bringing our horse friend back to life, now, is there? It was ready for the knacker's yard!" Nellie said with a chuckle.

Harry was at a loss as to what to do—but his clearly eccentric auntie had a point about the facts of the matter. The poor horse was no more—and had somehow become his meal against all British values, dining norms, and culinary propriety.

Harry thought about the dark stew he had enjoyed with its glistening pieces of carrot, shiny round green peas, and, of course, the chunks of meat bathed in gravy. He looked at what remained on his plate. He was hungry, the stew was tasty, and at this point it *would* be a pity to waste what was left. He reluctantly picked up his fork and, though somewhat disgusted with himself for enjoying it, finished up the stew on his plate. He felt torn between shock that a horse had been turned into a meal—and truly glad to have a meal that made him feel nourished and which eased the gnawing hunger pangs that had become the undercurrent of everyday life.

While part of him wanted to be angry that Auntie Nellie had procured and cooked horsemeat for him, he couldn't help but be impressed that she was resourceful in the mysterious ways of getting food in her larder that were hard to come by for just about everybody else. He knew that she had meant him no harm in feeding him her "special stew." Just the opposite.

Harry had to laugh to himself, too. Visits to Doncaster Place were never dull. It was a meal he would never forget. He vowed to never eat horse again, war or no war. Still, he was thankful that his auntie had shown enough care for his well-being to use the riches of her larder to feed him.

Doodle Bugs

A week after the Allies successfully landed on the beaches of Normandy in France in June 1944, the Nazis unleased a new kind of weapon against Britain—the *Vergultunswaffe— or Vengeance Weapon*. Launched by the *Luftwaffe* from Holland and northern France, this rocket-propelled flying bomb struck a new kind of terror into the lives of a war-weary Britain. They could be detected by radar, but not stopped—at least initially.

Their engines made a disturbingly loud, low, sickly-sounding fluttery vibrating sound as they flew, leading to their being nick-named buzz bombs or doodle bugs. The sound struck terror as they approached, but when they suddenly went silent it was worse. That meant that by design they had run out of fuel, then they randomly dropped from the sky, crashed, then exploded. Thousands were launched to drop on London. Others were directed to other targets around Britain.

It was a just past sunset on a warm summer evening. Harry and Tommy Jacques were outside in Moxon's Yard chatting about cricket and having a laugh, looking forward to a day when the war would end in victory and hopefully, Sheffield Wednesday would resume competing.

Most everyone else on Moxon's Yard was already inside readying themselves for bed. All was calm on Rawmarsh Hill. Suddenly, as Harry and Tommy continued their conversation, the sound everyone dreaded began to fill the air: A doodle bug was making its way right toward Rawmarsh. Quick thinking, Tommy Jacques didn't hesitate: He lifted Harry over one shoulder and made a run for it into the Waistnedges' house and headed back to the kitchen.

"Quick, get under this table!" Tommy urged Harry. The two pushed the chairs away and crouched under the kitchen table.

As they crouched there, the eerie and terrible vibrating sound of the doodle bug became louder and louder as its engine reverberated across the valley. Anyone and everyone in its path wished and prayed that it would keep going. Silence could mean death.

As the sound drew louder and closer still, Harry and Tommy held their breath, covered their ears, and squeezed their eyes shut. It was terrifying.

Fortunately, the doodle bug continued to cross over and passed Moxon's Yard. The two under the kitchen table heaved a sigh of relief—as did everyone else who were now behind its flight path.

But there may well have been more doodle bugs headed their way. Tommy and Harry decided to stay put, eventually nodding off and falling asleep under the table.

The next morning, Mr. Waistnedge was up early getting ready for work, came into the kitchen completely unaware that his kitchen had become a makeshift bomb shelter and that Harry and Tommy were there. As he walked in, the two stirred from under the table.

"Good morning Mr. Waistnedge," said Tommy with a perky tone and a broad smile as he popped his head out from under the table. The older man, startled, jumped backward, all but jumping out of his skin at the shock of hearing Tommy, then seeing the two young lads sheepishly start to come out from under the table.

"What on earth are you two lads doing 'ere?" he asked with a startled tone and baffled expression.

"We were outside last night when we heard the doodle bug come over. Your house was the closest shelter. I'm ever so sorry to frighten you," said Tommy earnestly. Harry nodded his head in solemn and contrite agreement.

"Never mind the bloody doodle bug, you two lads nearly killed me with shock!" said Mr. Waistnedge as his pounding heart thumped in his chest.

"We're ever so sorry," said Harry, seeing that his neighbor was visibly still in a state of shocked surprise. Then their neighbor began to calm.

"It's all right lads. Blimey, I don't know, it's a crazy time, it is. It's no way for all of us to have to live. No way for you two to have to live."

Then, after a moment of reflection, he began to chuckle. "I'm all right, lads. I'm glad you are, too. I can't say I'd do any different than you did in the circumstances. It's all right. I'm all right. You're good lads."

The three shook hands, then Mr. Waistnedge accompanied Harry and Tommy as they made their way out the Waistnedges' front door to home.

"Go home quick to your mothers so they don't find you not in bed and start to worry." Said Mr. Waistnedge.

With that, Harry and Tommy looked at him, then each other, and both laughed. Tommy headed left up to his house, and Harry headed to the right toward home. Both were glad to be safe and still have a home to go to after the terror of the previous night and the unintended shock they had struck into the heart of their groggy neighbor the morning after.

Tommy and Harry learned later in the day that the doodle bug had crashed in a field near Wentworth but not exploded. It was a dud—but had it worked it could have been tragic.

A Promise Betrayed

1945

With the war over, William was eager to return to Steel, Peech & Tozer at the earliest opportunity. He had put in two gruelling years down the pit. He was now 44 years old and the work that had been back breaking and gruelling as a younger man was even more so now. His knees were painful from crouching in the tight confines of the coal seam. He was beginning to feel old. He was ready to take advantage of the government's promise that if he went back to mining to support the war effort, he'd have a job to return to at the steelworks after the war was won.

There was an air of excitement in the Bailey household as William put on his best suit on a Monday morning to take the trackless to Rotherham and then over to Steelos, as he and his workmates called it, to arrange for his return to his former work.

"See you after school!" chirped Harry, having shared breakfast time with William and Edna before leaving for school. "Before you know it, no more pit clothes for you! Uncle Harold will be glad to see you back!"

William beamed with relief at the prospect of soon returning to work above ground. He rose and gave Edna a kiss on the cheek and Harry a warm pat on the back, then grabbed his cloth cap and headed out the door with a spring in his step to head to Rotherham.

William made his way along Sheffield Road and reached his destination. The mammoth steelworks was nearly a mile in length and with its chimneys firing away, was a massive sight to behold. It stood on the site of the former Roman fort at Templeborough—and had buildings on both sides of the River Don. He quickened his pace. He had been proud to work there, especially during the war effort, when Steelos' output of millions of pounds of ingots for munitions from anti-aircraft guns to machine guns. Before long he'd be back working with his brother-in-law and the thousands more mates he'd worked alongside before returning to the mine. True, it was like Hell's cauldron—all noise, intense heat, and sparks flying, but it was above ground and there was room to stand tall and move freely.

Upon arrival, William headed straight to the management offices to arrange for his return to work. He was directed to wait at a wooden bench outside the management office. He sat patiently for 15 minutes, then 30, then an hour. At last, an unsmiling manager popped his head out of the door to beckon him inside, failing to make eye contact with William: "Come this way Mr. Bailey" he said with a clipped efficiency and distinct lack of warmth in his tone. William rose and followed the man.

"Do sit down, Mr. Bailey," said the manager, still not making eye contact. He began to shuffle through some papers in a file, then pulling a document from it. "Yes—here it is! I see you chose to leave us to return to the mines—ah yes, that's right—because the government needed more miners. That's decent of you." His voice lacked sincerity. He dipped his pen into his inkwell, then began to scratch sentences onto the file.

"Yes, I went back down the pit two years ago," said William. He then added enthusiastically, "The government said there would be a job for me when the war ended."

"Well, yes, Mr. Bailey, that's right. You are entitled to a job here now that the war has been won."

William felt a small wave of relief.

"The thing is, Mr. Bailey," the manager continued, "we don't have a job for you at the same level as before. As you can imagine, while your decision to go down the pit again was an honorable one, of course we had to fill your job here. So yes, you are entitled to a job here now, but you'll need to start at the bottom again as I've no job to give you at the same role and pay as before."

William couldn't believe what he had just heard. He felt heat spread across his face. Speaking out in a hoarse, faltering tone, he said, "What's that?"

"Mr. Bailey, I understand that you chose to leave your work to fulfill your patriotic duty. That said, the government order was that there would be a job for you when you returned. It didn't say that it was THE SAME job you had. Do you understand me? You're going to need to start where we have one—and that's as a beginner."

William trembled with a mix of anger and frustrated humiliation before saying, "But I was led to understand that I could return to *my* job."

"Mr. Bailey, let me say this again, we are happy to take you back—but we're not obliged to put you back where you were if we have filled the job while you were away. Do you want the job I have available—or don't you?"

William squeezed the brim of the cloth cap he held in his now sweating hands. It was all he could do to contain his anger, anguish, and sense of betrayal. He had to do something to keep his emotions in check and his pride intact, then, reluctantly, hoarsely, he shook his head "Yes" to taking what he could get.

"Very good, then, Mr. Bailey. Welcome back! You can begin next week."

With that, the punctilious manager pushed papers toward William to sign that he agreed to return under the present conditions and wages lower than what he had earned when he left there two years. William quickly read the forms, then reluctantly penned his signature to the agreement. His normally beautiful penmanship showed the signs of a shaking hand. He couldn't look at the manager. He stood, picked up his cap, and turned to go. Inside, he felt like someone had delivered a hard kick to his gut.

When Harry came home that afternoon he walked in on an unsettling scene: William was bent over in his chair in a posture of defeat, his hands covering his face. Edna was seated across from him with the tell-tale remnants of shed tears showing on her flushed cheeks.

"Dad, mum, what's the matter?" asked an alarmed Harry as he quickly shut the front door and dropped his satchel by the front door. William was reeling with humiliation and couldn't look at his son. Edna dabbed her eyes with a well-wrung handkerchief and looked away toward the wall. Both parents were in a state of pained silence.

Harry drew closer to them and urgently asked again, "What's wrong? Dad? Mum? Tell me?!"

Edna was the first one to break the silence: "Your dad has been lied to about returning to the steelworks!"

"What do you mean?" Harry responded with alarm.

"He told them he was ready to return to his job—and they told him he could have a job, but not the same kind he had before. He's to start from the bottom and work his way up all over again—with the lower wages and sweeping of floors that comes with that!" Her voice broke and she fought back tears.

"Dad, how could they do this?" Harry asked, alarmed.

"They do whatever they like—that's how!" said William quietly, in a crest-fallen, resigned tone.

Harry's mind flooded with images of all the mornings over the past two years that William rose in the dark to go and work in the dark down the pit during the war, something he didn't want to do, but something he did anyway because his country needed him to do it. He remained silent for a while lost in thought, then solemnly and quietly said to his parents, "Dad, Mum, I can leave school and get a job. I'm not above going down the pit or working in the steelworks or a factory. I can help earn money."

William reeled quickly in his chair, then firmly gripped Harry's hand and looked him squarely in the eyes, saying with renewed fervor, "You're to finish your education Harry. You're to make something of yourself. You may not be above going down the pit, but I'll be damned if you do. I will have failed as a father if you follow in my footsteps. You *must* finish your education! Enough men in this family have gone down the mines for too long for too little. We've put up with too much for too long. *You will go to school!*"

Harry was speechless. No matter what, William and Edna placed his education above everything—even if it meant they would go further without than they already had. He thought of all they had given up for him—and the nights when Edna sat by the fire mending a ladder in her stockings or in a cardigan yet again while he studied up in his room—to save for what he needed. Harry's eyes filled with tears, which he fought mightily to avoid shedding. Then, involuntarily, he sobbed, part in sadness for his parents' struggles and part in relief that his parents believed his education was that important that he could stay in school. He hugged his dad tight, then turned to hug Edna.

William thought back to the time years when Harry was a little boy before the war, back when he struggled for months on end to find employment. He remembered the time Harry had sat on his lap and hugged him on the brutally cold day when he had desperately walked from pit to pit in the district, near to frostbite, seeking work without success.

Harry remembered back to the summer afternoons and evenings years before when William would sit outside with him, Derek, and Alan and, in between funny stories, answer their questions about life down the pit and then telling them that they weren't to go down the pit like he did. He thought at the time that William was joking—since all but a few of the men they knew were miners or steel workers. Now he knew that William was serious and determined that his son would be able to write another script for his own life.

The day that had started with such promise had taken a painful turn when William went to arrange his return to Steel Peech & Tozer. It had also crystallized for the family that Harry's education was more important than ever. They would sacrifice for it. William was adamant that Harry would have a chance of more choices and a better life—and his education was essential to making that possible.

The Enemy Comes to Church

1946

Greasborough Tops served more than one purpose during the war. Around the Big Bertha anti-aircraft guns, it provided much-needed farmland. The Ministry of Defence also established a prisoner-of-war camp there. First Italian, then German POWs were held there, housed in Nissen huts made of corrugated tin and wood. Those imprisoned here were considered to be of low risk. The Italian soldiers were even allowed to go into Parkgate on occasion, becoming a focus of much fascination as they peeked into shops. One afternoon Edna got something of a shock when she opened the front door, only to see a group of Italian soldiers had been brought to The Regal to see a film and queued outside the ticket window on Moxon's Yard.

Everyone in Rawmarsh was relieved to know that the hardened Nazi prisoners of war were mostly sent further North, where they were kept under an intensely watchful eye.

Among those held at Greasborough Tops, many had been young conscripts, barely 18, who had known nothing other than following orders and being told what to believe all their lives growing up under Nazism. Some had been 12 and 13 years old when the war began. Now they were just barely young men. As prisoners, they became farm hands, cultivating and harvesting desperately needed crops alongside English farmers. In spare time many took part in making toys for local children, one of the ways the camp staff kept the POWs occupied as it remained unclear as to when many would be allowed to return to Germany.

The brutality of the Nazis meant that the public's condemnation of them was understandable. A potent mix of hatred and fear had welled up in many local people over the course of the war—but now, as they became a more familiar sight and Britain and the Allies had won the war, there came to be more acceptance of the POWs as they contributed to farming, re-construction, and other urgently needed work to feed and re-build a battered Britain.

And so, on a spring Sunday morning in April, Harry and everyone present at St. Mary's was astonished when an orderly group of 30 German prisoners of war made their way into St. Mary's, led by a British Army sergeant from the camp. The enemy had come to church. Entering the church in two side-by-side lines of 15 soldiers, the POWs quietly filed into rows of pews set aside for their visit. Many were little more than 18 years old, maybe 20.

They were dressed in what they had: POW uniforms with large, red, circular patches on the backs of their shirts that made them easily identifiable. Their clothing reflected that fact that they had each been interrogated and graded on the extent of their Nazi loyalties before being sent to the camp: a white or gray patch meant that the prisoner had been determined to have no particular loyalty to Nazism or was not ardent in support of National Socialism. There were no prisoners with black patches—representing that they were committed Nazis, many of whom had been active in the Waffen SS. Those prisoners were imprisoned in Scotland's wildest, harshest landscapes where the possibility of escape was minimal.

Harry broke into a sweat under his cassock—and his heart thumped strongly in his chest. His eyes met Norman's, whose face equally registered a sense of shocked fascination and astonishment. All their pre-conceived notions of what the enemy looked like gave way to a picture before them far different than what they had imagined. These prisoners were in many cases little older than they were—young men who had experienced the "kill or be killed" brutality of war and who now faced great uncertainty about their futures and knew nothing about the welfare of their families. Some even had no desire to return to Germany if their homes were in the Soviet sector. The prisoners now in church were incapable of inflicting any further damage.

For the first time since the war began in 1939, Harry experienced a comforting wave of safety and security. It seemed to sweep through almost everyone gathered that morning—the pall of a menacing darkness and fear that finally giving way to light. Fear and hatred were exhausting. In a moment of grace, after close to six years of living in fear and loathing of the enemy, the defensive grip of animosity in Harry's heart melted away. He felt truly, deeply compassionate for these young men now far from their families, friends, homes, and a country now conquered and divided between the UK, US, France, and Soviet Union.

336

Looking into the faces and eyes of the soldiers for as long as he could without staring too long, Harry realized that in other circumstances many of them could easily have been his classmates, friends, and fellow choristers.

Reverend Scovell and Mr. Allott had known in advance that the prisoners would be present that morning, they had chosen a William Dunkerley hymn—one the choir had sung many times before. It took on new relevance for Harry after the encounter with the prisoners during the service:

In Christ there is no East or West,
in him no South or North,
but one great fellowship of love
throughout the whole wide earth.
In him shall true hearts everywhere
their high communion find,
his service is the golden cord
close-binding all mankind.
Join hands, disciples of the faith,
whate'er your race may be!
Who serves my Father as a son
is surely kin to me.
In Christ now meet both East and West,
in him meet South and North,
all Christly souls are one in him,
throughout the whole wide earth.

Harry knew that day that encountering the shared humanity of the enemy would be a defining moment of his life. He experienced a profound sense of the meaning of *loving thine enemy*. He felt free in a way he had not ever experience before. And it was an enormous relief after so many years at war.

Larry Leaves Mexborough

1946

With two years in at Mexborough and two more to go, Larry withdrew from school. He told Harry it was because his interests and energies had shifted away from studying to sport. But Harry wasn't convinced by Larry's explanation. A harsh reality lay underneath everything: Larry's parents' growing family was struggling and having a son at school when he could be earning money was a luxury they couldn't afford. At least that's the pressure Larry felt. And as Harry became more self-assured with every year at Mexborough, Larry never did feel like he belonged there. He was confident of his ability to do well out of school and wanted to do what he could to earn money to bring home to his family. He determined to find a job.

Harry felt sickened and pained by the turn of events. He and Larry were good friends: They laughed together, they understood each other. He saw Larry's clear intellect and appreciated his quick wit.

"Don't be upset, then, Harry," Larry, always one to put on a brave face, counselled his shaken friend on telling him the news. "It means no more coming to school not in proper uniform for me. No more sneers or dirty looks from anyone, no more feeling third rate in every class and hallway, on the cricket pitch. But you Harry, mark my words, you'll be fine. Don't go and give up because I have. You're made for something special, that much I know. And look here then: I'll hop the trackless to see you in Rawmarsh once I earn a few coppers!"

Harry smiled weakly at the plan, but in fact it was little consolation and he grieved to see his friend not able to continue at school with him. It hurt to think that, even with scholarships, Larry's chances and his own chances of a strong education matched to their abilities were so connected to the fortunes of their families. He felt sad for Larry and felt vulnerable himself.

On Larry's last day, the two friends walked out of school together. Larry's energetic gait was that of someone who had just put down a heavy burden. He walked along College Road to the trackless with Harry, then shook his hand enthusiastically. Harry boarded with other students headed to Wath and Rawmarsh, took his seat, and the doors snapped shut. Larry stood by on the road, beamed his infectiously warm big smile, and waved boisterously at Harry as the trackless began to move forward. Harry smiled, nodded, and returned the wave. In the flash of a moment he was transported back to the memory of meeting Larry on their first day at Mexborough: Out of uniform, striding up to him with plimsolls on his feet, intense, friendly, telling him that his real name was Doug but his mates called him Larry from the *Three Stooges*. Meeting him early on his first day made Harry more relaxed, made him smile. They were two bright, promising boys who all but immediately understood where they stood in the pecking order as new scholarship students. They were both glad of the opportunity to expand their horizons. They were both relieved to not have to go it alone.

Coming back to the present moment, Harry turned to look back through the windows. Larry waved some more, then turned to walk energetically toward home.

Amidst the after-school chatter of students, Harry's mind wandered as he stared out the window at the streets and valleys as the trackless made its way through a landscape predominated by slag heaps toward Rawmarsh. He realized that his own story could have been different, more like Larry's, if there were mouths to feed at home and even less space to share. While there were many days and nights when he wished he'd had a brother or sister, in this moment he realized an extra family member could have spelled the end of his education and no chance to go to Mexborough.

On returning to school the next week, Harry missed his friend greatly, noticing the void in classes, at meals, in banter between students at the Cabbage Patch. He had other friends, of course, but Larry's absence was like a void. Harry dug into his studies even deeper at Mexborough, into the chance to expand his horizons there. He did it for himself and, unconsciously, in part to honour his friend for whom poverty, lack of family support, and inadequate school support had eroded his confidence and been too much to bear to keep going.

Nearer, My God, to Thee

1946

"I'm off then, mum." said Harry as he picked up his ruck sack and headed out the door enthusiastically.

"Right then, lad, enjoy yourself and time with the other scouts." Edna called back from the kitchen, popping her head out to wave as Harry opened the front door and headed out to Moxon's Yard to meet up with Norman and the other scouts and leaders.

Edna smiled to herself as she thought about the chance Harry was getting to be outside on an adventure with the other Boy Scouts, hiking and exploring out in the fresh air in the moors. Soon they'd be pitching tents and roasting sausages over an open campfire in the evening, their relaxed faces glowing as they shared stories and laughed, imagining themselves to be in exotic places far away, perhaps like scouts' founder Lord Baden Powell himself—or Lawrence of Arabia.

Harry quickly made his way to the parish hall to drop off his sack and meet up with Norman, then the two were to drop by the rectory to collect some supplies from one of the new curates living in one of the flats there. Upon their arrival, the curate, who was one of the chaperones for the trip, greeted them at the door. "Hello lads. *So* glad you're here. I've got the cooking pots for the trip ready for you to take. Won't be more than a minute. Stand by, lads!"

Norman and Harry waited at the entry way as the curate disappeared, then returned with a box containing the pots. As he handed the box to the boys, he patted Harry on the back. "There, there's a good lad. *Well done*! I'll be over shortly to join up with everyone. Isn't this exciting?!"

Harry and Norman, pots in hand, headed across High Street toward the church hall. The other scouts were gathered there, all eager to head off for their camping adventure. Between them all they had assembled tents, food, and all the gear needed to house and feed the troop, scout master, and other adult leaders.

Everyone loaded onto a specially chartered bus. Most had not been on a bus like it since before the war, and its

344

spaciousness was part of the fun. They were now headed off to Walesby Forest in nearby Nottinghamshire. It was beautiful, a true get-away from the smog and grimy, narrow warrens of homes, slag heaps, and collieries that formed the landscape of their day-to-day lives.

The weather was perfect as they arrived at the forest. The verdant surroundings made Harry feel as if he were in another world all together. He breathed in the fresh air deeply.

The first order of the day was to set up camp. The troop were focused and serious, yet also full of banter and laughter as they unloaded the bus of supplies. They formed into teams, some to erect army-issue tents, others to set up their camp kitchen and build a bonfire to be lit at sunset. Yet others dug the necessary places for relieving themselves. Somehow, it all seemed effortless. It was the first time since the war had begun seven years earlier that the boys had been able to go on a camping trip. The mood was buoyant.

As the sun set and darkness set in, the bonfire was lit, and everyone tucked into supper—including tins of beans and kippers—plus bread toasted over the fire. Everyone looked forward to a "Knees Up Mother Brown" sing-along after a busy day of preparations.

Harry thought he was imagining it at first, but then he became certain that the new curate kept staring at him in a way that made him feel awkward. Deciding not to pay much notice, he re-focused on the group's activities.

As the weather grew cooler, Harry decided to go to his tent to find something warmer to wear. As he searched in his ruck sack, he suddenly realized that he was not alone. The curate had followed him and now stood at the tent's entrance.

"Hello there, Harry…can I help you find something?"

"Thank you, sir, no, I was just…" The curate had moved closer to him.

"Not to worry." said the curate in a tone that was meant to reassure Harry but sent off alarm bells in his mind instead. "What if we stay here, kneel down close together, and sing *"Nearer, My God, To Thee?"*

Harry began to feel terribly claustrophobic as he stammered, "No, thanks just the same…I need to…to get back to my friends..." Without delay he rushed past the curate out into the darkness, making his way quickly to the bonfire.

When he got there, Norman had been looking for him. "Where did you get off to, then, Harry?"

"Nowhere...just to our tent to look for something warmer to wear." Harry was tense, all the excitement of the day suddenly thrown into confusion in his mind.

"Are you all right?" Norman asked.

"Fine...I'm fine..." Harry replied flatly.

The remainder of the weekend Harry made a point of staying close to Norman and the other lads and avoiding any proximity to the curate. He didn't know what to make of their encounter in the tent, just that he wanted nothing to do with the man who held a position of respect in the community and the troop. The camping trip that he had so eagerly anticipated took a turn in a confusing direction he could never have anticipated.

John Fisher

1947

"Stand by, boys and girls, stand by! Look starboard!" boomed an enthusiastic Mr. John Fisher to Harry and the other student in Fisher's class as he had them peer "starboard" out the windows at the high seas beyond the school, "Be on the look-out for enemy submarines come to blow us out of the water!" This teacher was unlike any other Harry had known: He had his students up and out of their seats, rushing toward windows and imagining that they were at sea, then directing them "portside" to another part of the classroom and imagining the approach of an enemy submarine. It felt like theatre—and it got every student's attention.

Mr. Fisher, who taught English literature and writing, had returned to Mexborough after serving two year in the merchant marines. It was perilous work. Nazi submarines prowled for British and other Allied ships to torpedo. Thousands of crew and passengers died—and millions of tons of cargo were sunk. It was a difficult role for Fisher and all the men on board merchant ships crossing the stormy seas of war who served as the desperately needed lifeline between Britain and her allies.

Now, back in the classroom, it was almost as if he had not returned to the classroom but had instead transported his students to sea. Mr. Fisher was not one to mold himself into the set ways of teaching. Instead, he enlivened his students and the classroom with captivating tales of his time at sea. He loved the written word and brought literature to life and life into literature in the books and poetry they read and discussed. Harry had never had a teacher like him, someone who was so capable of bringing stories of the past into the present in such an engaging way. Until then Harry had preferred his science classes, but Mr. Fisher turned what had for him been a dry subject into a fascinating one. He inspired Harry to put in his best creative efforts in as a writer, something new—and it turned out, enjoyable—for him. Harry's natural writing gifts had yet to be fully revealed and he tended to delve on more into biology and chemistry, two subjects that were comfortable for him. But Fisher saw a spark in Harry, something well-worth giving voice to—and encouraged him

350

to be more confident in his unique perspective as a thinker, observer, and writer.

Harry was not alone in benefiting from this inspiring teacher's belief in his students. His classmate Ted Hughes was a gifted poet whose themes centered on nature and his rural childhood in the moors before moving to Mexborough. Mr. Fisher made time to guide Ted to develop his talents and see himself as having a future in the written word, supporting his work as editor of *The Dearne and Donne* student literary magazine.

Mr. Fisher had another positive effect on Harry: He helped him see the full value of embracing literature and story—to grow deeper in empathy and compassion through the characters he read about. While Harry had learned much from many teachers, Mr. Fisher had now influenced him in deeper ways than he had ever experienced intellectually before—and had treated him as an equal in his ability to cultivate the life of the mind and see himself as a capable, articulate thinker and writer. Most of all, Mr. Fisher had made Harry feel that he mattered as a person worth cultivating.

William's Work Accident

1947

Harry was in a buoyant mood as he made his way home from school after getting off the trackless. He and Norman Chappell had been telling jokes and chatting away on the ride from Mexborough—and Harry had earlier in the day enjoyed a deeper conversation with Ted Hughes as they surveyed the Cabbage Patch—or playing fields—at Mexborough in their roles as school prefects. Harry was now walking along High Street and just approaching the Regal when he noticed an uncharacteristically agitated Nanan looking up the street for him from the top of Moxon's Yard. Something had to be going on for her to make it to the top of the yard with her ulcerous, painful legs. Harry and Norman quickly ran up to her.

"Nanan, what's wrong?" asked Harry urgently.

Nanan was ashen faced, with neither her usual sparkling eyes nor smiling face whenever she saw Harry. "Oh Harry, I had to meet you before you got home...Your dad..." She began to as her voice began to shake, "Your dad—he has had an accident at work—the ends of three of his fingers were cut off...caught in one of the machines at t' steelworks..." The colour drained from Harry's face.

Nanan continued, "I didn't want you to walk into the house without warning...he's home now...bandaged up, in a lot of pain...and your mum is ever so upset.'

"Let's go!" said Harry. He and Norman helped Nanan, who needed a cane to walk, make their way back to number 21.When Harry opened the door, William was seated by the fire, his left hand wrapped in bandages.

William spoke with his eyes: He was in a great deal of pain given the number of nerve endings in fingers. The doctor had given him something for the pain. Edna took one look at Harry as he walked in, then began to sob.

"Dad!" Harry cried out as he threw down his school satchel and rushed to William's side, "Dad! Oh God!"

Harry looked back at Nanan, whose own mind was flooded with flashbacks of all the men, women, and children she knew in her life who had suffered all manner of injury doing their jobs. She remembered kissing William's delicate fingers when he was a bonny baby. Now they were maimed. If injury was to be expected in families like hers, it didn't hurt any less to witness when it did happen.

Finally, William spoke up, his voice hoarse but proud: "It could have been worse…it could have been my whole hand—or it could have been down the pit…I'm alive. I can go back to work again once everything heals."

Harry took one look at both of his parents, who suddenly seemed so much older to him, and at Nanan, who had experienced and witnessed so much hardship in her seven decades so far. They deserved something better. He determined to keep up his studies to have a better chance to help them. He wanted to help them more than anything.

Just then, they all heard a steady, kindly, and familiar voice: Dr. O'Connell had come around to check in on William. He had been contacted by the steelworks' clinic about William's accident.

"May I come in and check on Mr. Bailey?" said the doctor as he lifted his hat to greet Nanan at the door.

"Dr. O'Connell, oh yes, please, do come in!" said Nanan with a slight dip in her stiff knees in deference to the doctor who had cared for the Baileys for so many years, most of the time seeing to Edna through various ailments.

He came in and sat in the seat Edna pulled up for him to sit by William. "Mr. Bailey, I am ever so sorry that this has happened to you. We must now make sure that your hand can heal fully and that you do not get an infection of any kind." He took a look at the bandaged hand, then continued, "May I take a look?" William nodded his consent. Dr. O'Connell gently unwrapped the outer bandages, getting down to the gauze. "We'll need to keep this clean and dry," the doctor continued. "I'll need you to come around to my surgery tomorrow and we'll take a look again, keep an eye that it's healing properly, and change this gauze and bandages." William nodded his understanding. Harry looked on, grateful and fascinated by the doctor's hearthside manner. He admired him. Dr. O'Connell in turn could not but notice that Harry was growing up to be a fine young man. How far he had come from his perilous birth.

After spending 20 minutes with the family, Dr. O'Connell knew that it was time to take his leave to that the traumatized family could begin to come to terms with William's situation and heal itself.

Just as Dr. O'Connell was leaving, Uncle Leonard arrived from a trip to the chemist, where he had been instructed to buy supplies for tending to William's injury. He, too, looked upset at what had happened to his older brother.

"Mr. Bailey," said Dr. O'Connell to Leonard, "Your brother has been through too much today, but it's a very good thing that you are here to help." Leonard tipped his cap at the doctor. The two men shook hands, and Dr. O'Connell headed out to continue his rounds.

In what had been a painful day for William and all the family, the healing began with the comfort of knowing that he was surrounded with love. For Harry, it furthered his resolve to do his best at school. Somehow, he was determined to help his parents. Somehow.

Carbon Urinate Gas

1947

NEVER weather-beaten sail more willing bent to shore,
Never tired pilgrims' limbs affected slumber more,
Than my wearied sprite now longs to fly out of my troubled breast:
O come quickly sweetest Lord, and take my soul to rest!
--Thomas Campion

It was a late winter afternoon. Harry, Norman, and Horace, who took a break from his medical school studies to sing, had just joined in a special choir practice for a funeral to be held the next day. Now finished, at Frank Pickering's request, the three had agreed to clear up and turn off the lights after everyone else in the choir had left.

They went about their duties with efficiency, then headed outside through the vestibule, turning toward the church hall and Devil's Side of the church yard. Horace realized then that he had left his woollen scarf in the church. "I'll be right back," he said to Harry and Norman before turning back to collect it.

Harry and Norman stood in the church yard for a few moments while Horace went to fetch his scarf. Their curiosity was raised when they noticed that the lights were on in the church hall.

"What's going on in there, then?" inquired Norman with a hint of mischief.

"Dunno" said Harry, "It's not scouts. We're outside here!"

"Maybe Girl Guides then?" posited Norman.

"Oooh, now there's an idea." said Harry. "Let's go in the cellar and see if we can hear from there. We'll know soon enough if there are lasses upstairs."

The two of them quietly made their way into the basement of the church hall for a listen. Norman fumbled for a light switch, then turned it on. Roaring away before them was the building's coal-fire furnace.

"Let's have a look then," said Harry, curious to see inside the furnace.

The boys opened up the furnace door to the sight and intense heat of the red-hot coals.

Norman spotted a coal bucket and a shovel next to the furnace. "Come on then, let's fill this bucket up with hot coals..."

Harry eagerly agreed. Now they were there it was something to do.

Norman carefully retrieved some of the hot coals from the furnace and dropped them into the bucket. They glowed brightly and the space began to quickly fill with acrid coal smoke, making the boys cough.

"Crikey!" Harry exclaimed, "We've got to put these coals out. We'll burn the place down and they stink something horrid."

"But we've not got water!" observed Norman just short of panicked. "What are we to do, then?"

The boys stared at each other, hoping each would have an answer.

"Well, can't we just shove 'em back in the furnace?" thought Harry quickly.

"No, they may fall to the floor—and that bucket handle is too hot to handle." Replied Norman. The cellar was getting smokier, smellier, and the coals were still red hot.

And in an instant, Norman had a plan:

"Right then, unzip your fly. We'll piss in the bucket! We've brought our own fire hoses!"

Harry, whose eyes were tearing up from the smoke by this point, wasted no time in joining in with Norman in producing their fire extinguishing gear. The two relieved themselves into the bucket.

"Ooh, that's better. 'P for relief.' I've been holding that for a while." laughed Harry.

The red-hot coals were being quickly doused—and the boys were about to congratulate themselves on their ingenuity.

But just as quickly as the pee rained down on the coals and they were extinguished, hot steam began to rise toward them—and with it a hideous acrid stench of carbon mixed with urine.

"Bloody hell!" Norman and Harry exclaimed in horror in unison. The two quickly made their way for the cellar steps and door—zipping up their flies as they scrambled—and as the steam-carried stench wafted through the cellar and continued to foul the air.

Horace had been waiting patiently in the church yard, having seen the cellar door ajar, the light on, and figuring that Harry and Norman might be having a look around the cellar for some reason. He was now surprised to see the two shove open the door and scramble into the church yard. Once outside the two gulped in fresher air, then burst into a peal of laughter at their foolishness. Horace was about to ask, "What on earth…?"

But within seconds Harry and Norman realized that they weren't the only ones fleeing into the church yard. The carbon-urine-stench from the steam had risen upward from the cellar into the church hall, quickly polluting the air with the foulness and disrupting the weekly Mother's Union meeting. As Harry, Norman, and Horace watched in shocked amazement, the church hall's thick wooden doors burst open wide as close to three dozen mothers with babes in arms and toddlers in tow fled screeching in haste from the building. Some were covering their mouths and noses with handkerchiefs; others had wrapped coats around their faces and their children's' faces covering all but their eyes and foreheads. Some of the children kept their faces pressed up against their mothers' thighs to try to block the stench from reaching their nostrils.

Horace put two and two together. Whatever Harry and Norman had done in the cellar had set off this commotion. He knew they needed to quickly find cover, for Hell would have no fury like mothers forced outside with their children in such a way. "Come on!' Horace called out to Harry and Norman. With the general commotion and chatter of the mass exodus from the meeting as cover, Harry, Norman, and Horace took advantage of the darkening skies of sunset and large Victorian tombs around them and crept quietly into the shadows, where they hid behind one of the larger tombs in the church yard. There they could only wait and hope not to be seen.

With the Mother's Union meeting at an abrupt end and the women recovering from their steam-driven ordeal, the various mothers loudly posited a range of theories as to what could have caused such a situation: "I'll be sure to let Frank Pickering know straight away. Something must have died in the heating system—a mouse or rat?" "Or perhaps the coal was off somehow?" said another. "I never! Dear me today!" declared the group leader. A chorus of several "Dear me today!" declarations followed from the group.

In the minutes that followed, given the darkening skies and damp, cold air, the mothers began to wrap up their discussion and leave with their children in twos and threes toward the trackless and neighboring streets, some pushing prams, others walking hand-in-hand with toddlers, all glad to be away from the mysterious stench and its shock to the nostrils. The meeting leader, after cautiously sniffing inside the hall, then bravely ventured in to switch off the lights before returning to close the doors. She continued to shake her head in disbelief as she headed toward High Street.

Prudently, Harry, Norman, and Horace, eager to come out of the situation alive, stayed hidden behind the tombstone until all signs of mothers with young children were out of sight.

They repressed their laughter as best they could, daring not look at each other, then took turns popping their heads up to survey the church yard.

"The coast is clear!" whispered Harry at last, half seriously, half mischievously.

"What are we going to call that nasty mix?" pondered Norman with a giggle.

"Well, coal and pee—that's carbon and urine…" replied Harry, thinking about his school chemistry lessons.

"Good," chimed in Horace. "We'll call it Carbon-Urinate Gas!"

The friends laughed, shuddered from the chill in the air, then, after peeking cautiously around the church yard one more time to make sure no one was around, pulled up the collars on their coats around their ears to make it more difficult to see their faces. They then headed in the shadows toward their respective homes like three spies in a Hitchcock film, splitting off in three ways—Harry across the street toward the Earl Grey, then left toward Moxon's Yard; Norman toward the Earl Grey, then right to Rockliffe Road; and Horace, who stayed on the church side of the road making sure the coast remained clear for the other two boys, before slipping down High Street past the Cenotaph toward Parkgate and Ashwood Road.

"Not Good Enough for My Daughter"

1947

Harry took a quick glance at his image reflecting on the windowpanes in his room. Satisfied, he adjusted his tie a bit at his neck, then ran downstairs. He'd made plans to meet Clara Hook and had dressed in his new blazer and dress shirt to meet her at her house before heading together to the dance hall at the swimming baths.

All set and ready to go, he ran down the stairs and headed to the open front door. William was outside having a chat with Frank Pickering. It was a perfect late spring evening and most families on the yard were taking full advantage of the fine weather.

"Dad, I'm headed out now. I'll see you and mum later, then!"

"Right son, enjoy yourself," replied William, happy to see Harry full of excitement about heading out with a lovely girl.

"You'll be the most handsome lad at the dance hall!" added Frank Pickering with a smile and pat on Harry's back. Harry blushed crimson, then smiled.

With that, he said his good-byes and made his way to the Regal's front entrance ticket booth facing High Street to see Edna, who had a new job there as a ticket seller. Edna thrived on the social interactions that came with the exchange of shillings and pence for tickets. It opened a wider world up to her. Clearly getting out and seeing more people was good for her. She clearly relished her new role, one which Harry had noticed lifted her spirits to reveal a sunnier and more optimistic woman than he had known for most of his life.

The ticket booth was quiet when Harry approached the window. Edna took one look at her son dressed up for a special night out, then beamed, "You look right handsome, son. With your hair combed that way you're a proper Cary Grant or Stewart Granger. You could be in pictures yourself!"

Harry blushed yet again and enjoyed the thought that she thought that he looked the part of a film star. "Ta, mum!" he said to Edna. As patrons approached the window, Harry flashed a quick smile at Enda, waved, then turned to head out to collect Clara and head to the dance hall for the evening. Edna smiled with pride as she watched him go.

After a 15-minute walk up and past the swimming baths, Harry arrived at the Hooks' house, opened the garden gate, and made his way up the flower-framed walkway to the front door and rang the bell. Expecting Clara to answer, Harry was surprised when Mr. Hook did so instead—and he wasn't smiling.

He wasted no time in saying what he had to say: "Look here, lad, it's a fine thing that you know my daughter from youth group. She's a beautiful lass. I understand that she's attractive to you and so many of the lads around here."

Harry began to feel a deep unease from the older man's tone as he spoke. "The fact is, as Clara's father, it's up to me to make sure she associates with only suitable young men." He looked Harry up and down for a moment, then continued, "I'll get down to brass tacks. No daughter of mine is going to go out with the likes of you. Isn't your father…" He paused, then continued with deep, disdainful emphasis on, "…a *miner?*"

Harry began to feel confused. He and Clara had gone out many times in previous months—and Harry had been to her house for tea along with others from church. They enjoyed time together—at youth group, at the cinema, at the dance hall. Their friends thought of them as a couple.

The confusion clearly showed on Harry's face. Mr. Hook took the opportunity to pounce further: *"You're not good enough for my daughter. Full stop.* You're working class. You're not to show up here anymore—and I won't tolerate your being anywhere near my daughter. You're to stay clear of her." The aggression in his words was palpable.

With that, in a final gesture of bombast, he puffed out his chest, glared at Harry, stepped back into the house, then slammed the door shut.

Harry was stunned. Mr. Hook's words stung more harshly than any physical blow. He was beyond confused. He had known Clara for year from both church and Haugh Road School. He had been welcomed in their home before along with others from the church youth group. But now, there on his own, the Hook patriarch made sure to put a stop to it.

.

Not sure what else to do, Harry turned and walked away from the house, feeling dazed and blind yet also feeling as if thousands of eyes were focused menacingly on him from the windows of the houses surrounding him and anyone within his view on the street. Something else flooded back involuntarily from long before: The painful memory of his bicycle fall as a child and Mrs. Marriott's hissing disdain as he lay on the pavement tangled on top of his bicycle with bloodied knees and elbows: *"Get out of my way, miner's son!"*

Snapping himself back again to the present moment, Harry, once on the street, turned to look back toward the house, catching sight of the lace curtains pulled to one side as Clara peeked out of the sitting room window toward him, then, seeing that he had seen her, quickly letting the curtain fall shut and disappearing.

And just as Harry turned to walk away, he looked ahead and, in disbelief, saw Alistair Grimesthorpe, who both he and Clara knew from church and who went to public school. Tall, self-assured, richly well-dressed, he was clearly prepared up for an evening out with a special girl—and headed straight to the Hooks' home. Alistair had always been skilled in making not-so-subtle calls outs to heighten class distinctions with boys like Harry. A sly comment here, a disapproving look there, compliments that felt more like insults, an insolent tone. Now he had his eyes on the butcher's daughter. Mr. Hook would certainly approve of Alistair as more than "good enough" for his Clara, since the young man's father was a clergyman, a cut above. In a flash, Alistair gave Harry the smug look up and down, nodded sharply at him more as a warning shot than a gesture of civility, and without a word walked straight past Harry, continuing on toward the Hook home with a confident, self-satisfied gait.

Harry was deeper in shock as the full realization of it all hit him. No matter his talents, his accomplishments, his character, how much Clara meant to him, her father had cut him down in an instant, treating him as all but worthless.

Waves of psychic and physical pain washed over him. He was stung by the cruelty and humiliation. He didn't want to go home and explain anything to them or the friends he expected to see at the dance. So instead Harry walked, walked, and walked some more, each step a labor—no longer noticing the fine weather and averting his eyes from passersby, as if they were in the know on the Hook patriarch's verbal evisceration of him.

After walking for a long time, Harry was drawn to the dance hall he had planned to go to with Clara. Instead of going inside where he would be bound to meet friends, he stayed back from the building, heading to a secluded bench, where veiled in its shadows, he could avoid being seen by anyone who knew him. He listened to the band music, bursts of applause between dances, and the hum and gaiety of happy voices punctuated with occasional laughter. It was both too close yet all too far away at once. He should have been among those having a grand time—but he wasn't. He was locked in the private hell of his wounded feelings. He had expected that he and Clara would have a lovely evening, but now instead he wanted nothing more than to disappear. To escape Rawmarsh. To escape all that kept him and all the people there locked in the suffocating, un-bending social hierarchy. To escape all the labels that came with it. To experience some kind of freedom he didn't even know how to name.

And as he hung his head down lost in his thoughts, he soon heard the all too familiar and delightful, hearty laugh of Clara, pretty as ever and all dressed up for a special evening, hanging on Alistair's arm and every word and headed into the dance hall. Harry moved further away into the shadows, loosened his tie, then wept.

Dusk turned to blackness as Harry watched couples coming and going from the swimming baths dance hall. The gas lights on the street and the occasional head lamps of the trackless cast a glow up High Street and Haugh Road. It was a perfect evening for romance—yet he couldn't have felt more desolate. At long last, the music stopped and the dance hall emptied slowly and steadily as the crowd dispersed, the musicians lit cigarettes at the front door as they departed with their instrument cases, and someone switched off the lights, whistling *Don't Sit Under the Apple Tree* as he then made his way toward Victoria Park and Silver City.

When all fell quiet Harry made his way home. Edna and William had made plans to meet friends at the Star Inn earlier in the evening and would now be home in bed. He couldn't bear the idea of their seeing him or asking him about his evening out. He was grateful that the houses were in darkness when he turned onto Moxon's Yard. He slipped alongside the

Regal, past the neighbors' doors, and quietly let himself inside once home.

He cut through the dark front room, through the kitchen, and slowly climbed the stairs hoping not to hit the creaky floorboards, then slid quietly into his room. He closed the door, pulled off his tie, loosened his collar, then poured water into the bowl on his dresser from the jug, then splashed his face with the cold water. Without removing his jacket or shirt, he dropped onto the mattress on his bed and stared toward the into the darkness that surrounded him. His heart beat hard in his chest. He heard the whistle and rumbling of a train in the distance. He sweated, tossed, and turned for what seemed like hours, then finally fell asleep.

The next morning was Sunday. Harry stirred, rose, and splashed his face with cold water again. All the feelings of anguish and pain flooded back to him. Mr. Hook's stinging words kept repeating over and over again in his head. *"You're a miner's son. You're not good enough for my daughter."* What did Clara think about it? Did she want what her father wanted? His one hope was that she would stand up for Harry, for both of them, and convince her father to let them be together. But clearly, she hadn't. Then he thought of how Alistair Grimesthorpe was clearly expected at the Hook house shortly after him. Clara had clearly been expecting him—and, strangely, done nothing to let Harry know their evening outing together and everything else was off. Had she planned it so that her dad would rip into him and so he'd see Alistair?

Harry had little time to think further on the situation: He had bells to ring and choir to go to—and as head choir boy he had the responsibility of showing up and setting a good example, no matter how wretched he felt. He washed up and changed his clothes, made breakfast as Edna and William slept in, then headed over to St. Mary's to robe up for choir, then headed up the steps to the tower to prepare to ring.

Harry ran into Frank Pickering, who was preparing the church for the service. Frank saw in an instant that Harry's usual spark was nowhere to be seen. He lay down the box of candles in his hands and walked over to the now handsome young man he had seen grow up before his eyes. "Harry, you look as if a ton of bricks has fallen on you this morning," he said, seeing no reason to be anything but direct. "What's up, lad?"

Harry shrugged his shoulder and looked awkwardly at the floor between them.

"Come lad, when I see a crestfallen young man as you are now, I can't help but want to help."

"It's nothing…" said Harry, unconvinced by his own statement.

"It's summat, good man." said the kindly neighbor.

Harry thought quietly for a moment, then raised his eyes from their focus on the floor. He looked pained indeed, but did his best to keep his composure as he quietly said, "What does it take around here to be seen as mattering?"

"Mattering? *You*? *Harry Bailey*? Oh lad, you are a credit to us all, you are! How did you get the idea that you don't matter?" Pickering asked.

"It seems that I'm not good enough for a girl I like. Her dad told me as much, told me to shove off—that I was worthless because I'm a miner's son. She's seeing a vicar's son—public school and all."

"Well I'll be…" said Pickering, taking it all in, then saying, "It's 1947, we've fought and won yet another bloody war, and somebody has the nerve to tell you that? You're not only good enough for his daughter, but you're more than good enough. Don't you pay him no mind. He's not worth it."

"But I can't help but feel like he kicked the stuffing out of me." Harry replied.

"He doesn't know what to do when someone with as much intelligence, natural talent, and good character as you have comes along. Your dad was a miner, now he's a steel worker—so what? If I am right on the father in question, he's a butcher—slaughters pigs for a living—not the Earl Fitzwilliam! There's many of us who have crawled and scraped each day to survive. And I didn't lose a leg in t' Great War for the likes of him to be a bully to the likes of you now. Your dad is not only a brave, good man, he's a fine gentleman. I've known him since he were a scrawny tyke and he's a credit to us all."

"He is…it's just…why do some people…why do some people…" Harry's voice trailed off, then re-focused. He looked straight into Frank Pickering's eyes. "I don't know what will happen next, but I am proud of my dad."

Pickering reached out to give Harry a re-assuring pat on the back. "Look 'ere, Harry! You've had the stuffing knocked out of you there's no denyin' but know that there are so many of us here who know you'll succeed. I know you will."

"Ta, then…" said Harry, feeling better for having confided in his neighbor.

Just then Harry's friends arrived from the vestry as if on cue to prepare to head up to the bell chamber.

"Thanks, again," Harry said to Frank, who responded with a knowing, kindly wink.

The boys headed up the 60-plus steps to the bell chamber to prepare to ring. The concentration of ringing the changes and the good company of the other ringers helped Harry focus on something other than the pain he had been experiencing since the night before. He tugged at the rope in turn with an added intensity, then, as so many times before when the service processional was imminent, Harry, Norman, Horace and all the ringers who sang in the choir sped down the narrow spiral steps of the bell tower to grab their music and line up for the procession.

Harry realized that he'd likely have to see Clara and her family at church. The thought of being anywhere near her— or her father—set him off stinging anew. Frank Pickering, ever perceptive, realized the situation, and just as the organ music began for the processional hymn, moved up alongside Harry and whispered gently, "Chin up Harry. If any heads are to be down, let it be theirs."

Harry took his first steps in the procession, buffeted forward to the altar by the choir in motion. He stared straight ahead at the stained glass over the altar, passed by where the Hooks sat, and took his own seat in the choir stalls. He kept focused on the organist, choirmaster, and his music, avoiding any and all eye contact with the family—and somehow made it through the service. He only hoped that he could make it through subsequent Sundays, too.

The Cycle Broken

1948

Mexborough School was abuzz as the A-level examinations came in. Harry was all nerves as he jostled into the crowd to see the posting with his results. Finally, he saw them: Higher School Certificate in Science. An enormous sense of relief and happiness filled his being. He had passed.

Harry was offered acceptance to the University of Nottingham to study Zoology. He was elated—and couldn't wait to share the news with William, Edna, Nanan, Horace, Uncle Harold, and all the family and friends who had helped him and believed in him. Now he had a chance.

His friend Ted Hughes had passed his A-level exams with flying colours—and been accepted to Cambridge University.

Harry, Ted, and the other male students would go into military service for two years, then join their respective universities. Female students would have a well-earned chance to pursue their intellectual interests and own career interests, too, as places opened for them to go on to university.

Three years after the war had ended—despite all the shortages and hardships that continued—change was in the air. Coal miners' and steel workers' children—working class children—could aspire to study and pursue professions that had been closed to them or, in a rapidly changing world, had not even existed only a few years before. It was uncharted territory for these students and their families—and it was a chance they were eager to seize. A new, wider world largely unknown to them awaited them. It was both daunting and exciting.

News of Harry's positive exam results spread quickly throughout the family and up and down Moxon's Yard. Grandad Dyson, of all the members of the family, put on his best suit, picked up his silver-tipped cane, and paid a visit to his grandson, not so much to congratulate him, 'though he was in his heart deeply proud of Harry without saying so, but to be in the presence of someone who had accomplished what in his own youth was simply the stuff of outlandish dreams, "not knowing one's place," and simply out of the question.

Uncle Harold and Auntie Kath, who had supported Harry and his parents in the darkest hours of failing his eleven-plus exam, were so glad to congratulate him, too. For the older members of the family, something profoundly important was happening: Their children and grandchildren were finally breaking free of the lack of opportunity, the miseries of being born into the bottom rungs of society, the cruel trap of being judged, kept in their place, and scorned for being working class, the trap of some others in equal misery trying their level best to take anyone down a peg if they showed any promise or ambition.

There would be much more to overcome, but now Harry at least had a chance—and the family collectively committed in their hearts without saying as much that they would do all they could to help him soar.

For everyone in the family, this instinct was love unspoken, it was humiliation and despair overcome. Harry had been willing to do his part, and they would do theirs for him.

For King and Country

1948

Edna peered into Harry's room wistfully. How could it be that the son she had given birth to with such difficulty and peril 18 years previously was now packing up a duffle bag and preparing to head to London as an army private? How had that little baby boy gone from that to a clever boy who loved to read and learn, who had a gift for singing, for making friends and engendering support and loyalty, who had made such good friends in Horace and Norman? She thought of the sometimes seemingly endless nights, weeks, and months of nights the family spent in the Anderson shelter, when Harry, Derek, and Alan were brave and calm, even laughing at times as William told them stories to keep their spirits up? It all seemed like a strange dream now.

After one more breakfast at the kitchen on Moxon's Yard, Harry made his way to the Parkgate & Rawmarsh rail station platform to wait for the North Midland Railway train that would take him to London and the British Army national service that awaited him as Private Harry Bailey. The trip would take him the furthest away from home in his life so far. He was both nervous and excited to see the great capital city and the wider empire and world it stood in the center of.

Everything that had been the backdrop of his life until then suddenly came into sharp focus around him: The bell tower of St. Mary's, the smokestacks billowing coal smoke from the blast furnaces at the nearby Parkgate Iron & Steel Works, and the rail station itself—the launching point for the family and church youth group trips to the North Sea at Scarborough and Whitby and with Edna and William to Blackpool on the Irish Sea.

Harry placed his duffel bag down, then looked up the long lines of track heading in two directions, then began to survey the platform and station itself, noticing details he had never fully taken in before. Then he noticed another young man, this one in an army officer's uniform. To his shock, he realized it was Alistair Grimesthorpe—who had been the focus of Clara Hook's attention after the painful exchange Harry had with her father. Involuntarily, all the painful emotions flooded back. He fought hard within himself to push them out of his mind.

Harry quickly pivoted to walk in the opposite direction on the rail platform from his nemesis. If the two actually came face to face, he knew that as a private he would be obliged to salute anyone in the uniform of a military officer. That was the last thing he would ever want to do, especially in his final moments in Rawmarsh. London and army barracks on Millbank were to be his home for the foreseeable future.

Alistair, likely having seen Harry, this time did something decent, whether he meant to or not: He turned to move away from him up the platform. The two ignored each other.

On schedule, the train rumbled, whistled, and billowed its way toward the station, then stopped. Passengers, porters, and a conductor all set into motion getting off and getting on the train, like something from a film Harry had seen at The Regal. He saw the Royal Mail being loaded, too.

As usual, the train had first-and third-class cars, no second-class ones. Harry boarded the train in a third-class car to the back, hauling his duffle bag as he stepped up, made his way down the narrow aisle, then slid open the door to a compartment with an open seat. Alistair, meanwhile, had headed in the opposite direction toward the front, leather suitcase in hand, and boarded a first-class car on the same train. The two never saw each other again. And as the train pulled away from the station, Harry realized that they were both leaving Clara behind. He doubted Alistair would miss her—and he had determined to move on with his own life without her. After having the choice of two different young men in her life, in the end she was left behind by both. She, too, would need to navigate new stages of life.

Harry looked out the window as his grayish surroundings and the still burned-out hulks of war-bombed buildings and streets became a shrinking backdrop as new sights loomed larger. He was starting a new chapter away from the slag heaps and the mines, and steel works that had for so many years defined not only his life but those of his parents, uncles and aunts, cousins, grandparents, and just about everyone he knew in the Rother Valley.

Before long the train entered the countryside of Derbyshire and where he was headed: to London to join the army medical corps, where he would train as a radiology tech and, perhaps be sent overseas. Britain had new challenges as the Soviet Union strengthened, the vast British Empire—the "pink parts of the map" he had studied in school—were breaking off as independent nations. The beginnings of a new world order were taking shape. If all went well, two years later Harry would continue his education at university. But that still seemed like a century away—still all but a dream—except it was one that Horace had proven was possible by achieving his dream of becoming a doctor. For now, Harry was embarking on a new life away from Rawmarsh, Rotherham, Sheffield, and all he knew from living for 18 years in the West Riding.

Harry both dreaded and looked forward to what lay ahead for him in London. One thing was certain: Life was taking him in directions that neither his father nor grandfathers could ever have aspired to for themselves at his age. The brutal cycle was broken. Now was his chance. But first it was his turn to serve for King and Country.

Epilogue

1948 - Present

Harry Bailey

Harry Bailey entered the British Army in 1948 as a private, serving in the army medical corps based at Millbank Barracks in London. His bed was a relic left over from the days of the Crimean War of the 19th century. It didn't take long for his fellow recruits—mostly from East London—to realize that they could yank the ends of the bed frames from both ends so that the mattress of the person in the bed would fall to the floor. One drill sergeant told Harry during uniform inspection that he looked like "shit with string tied around the middle."

Harry lived in the heart of the capital—a quick walk, underground, or bus ride to London's great cultural religious, political, and artistic institutions including the Tate Gallery, Westminster Abbey, the Houses of Parliament, and St. Paul's Cathedral. Among the highlights of his time in London, he frequented Evensong choral services at Westminster Abbey, then dashed for the bus to make it to St. Paul's Cathedral for the Evensong service that started there one hour later. London might as well have been another planet for the boy from Moxon's Yard. He loved it.

He trained as an army medical corps radiology technician there before being assigned to the remote Yorkshire outpost base at Catterick, North Yorkshire. In sharp contrast to London, there was little to do there in any free time. The godsend of his days was the supply of newspapers and magazines provided for soldiers by the Salvation Army.

Promoted quickly, Corporal Harry Bailey left the army in 1950 at 20-years old. Rather than studying Zoology at University of Nottingham as planned when he left Mexborough, with Horace's guidance he instead applied to and was accepted at Sheffield University's School of Medicine. Horace, in reverse order to Harry, went to medical school first, then the army before marrying and starting a family. Harry fulfilled his military service first, then went to medical school. Harry never saw Horace again after the late 1940s. The two great friends lost touch as they both moved away from Rawmarsh and into different stages of their lives.

While studying at Sheffield, Harry met Kathleen, the love of his life in the university's madrigal group. They married in 1956 despite controversy covered in the press when my mother's scholarship was threatened if she married. Upon completion of his residency, my dad took a one-year residency in Newport, Rhode Island, USA, traveling to New York on the *Ìle de France* in 1957. My mother followed on the same ship a month later after completing her job as a teacher of music and French in Sheffield. Harry went on to complete a residency at the New England Deaconess Hospital in Boston—a Harvard Medical School teaching hospital—before joining the hospital staff. In addition to specializing in radiology in both hospital and private practice, he lectured at the medical school and guided a generation of radiology residents and contributed research to medical journals, specializing in diabetes-related radiology.

I was the middle of three children born to my parents. We grew up just outside of Boston in Westwood, Massachusetts from 1962-1977 before moving to Chestnut Hill in Brookline. Our house there had seven bathrooms—the significance of which was totally unknown to me at the time, but which must have been outlandish to my dad, given the physical conditions of his life on Moxon's Yard.

Throughout my childhood my father cultivated and energetically pursued his passion for gardening and raising orchids. He noticed that when he brought blooming ones to the hospital, his often-terminally-ill patients brightened up on seeing the beautiful blooms. He built two greenhouses to house his collection of a few hundred orchids, many exotic species of which he imported from Barbados and England.

Barbados became a second home of sorts to our family: We made multiple trips there together between the late 1960s and early 1980s and my parents acquired property there. My dad met one of his most treasured life-time friends there—Iris Bannochie—whose Andromeda Gardens were a magnet for horticulturalists and tourists alike and is now part of the Barbados National Trust. They met at a Barbados Orchid Society meeting. When my dad introduced himself as Dr. Harry Bailey, Iris nearly passed out. Her deceased first husband, much beloved, was named Dr. Harry Bayley; There is an observatory on Barbados in his honor. The meeting was the beginning of a beautiful friendship between our families.

We came close to moving to Barbados during a particularly harsh New England winter. Another friend in Barbados—one of my dad's former patients—had offered to sell him a lot next to his overlooking Bridgetown Harbour a few years earlier. My dad wrote to say he'd buy the lot, only to learn it had recently been sold.

In 1981, dis-enchanted with the politics of his career at a Harvard teaching hospital with the sometimes cut-throat ambition that flew in the face of the Hippocratic Oath to "Do no harm," he wanted a change. After years of little exposure to the sun between his dark morning and evening commutes and workdays spent in the dark room reading x-rays—Harry followed a Canadian friend's example and joined the United States Navy Medical Corps. He was first offered and turned down a posting to a small hospital at Guantanamo Bay, Cuba. He was soon after offered a posting to the U.S. Naval Hospital at Balboa Park in San Diego, California. My parents moved to Coronado, California and lived by the Pacific Ocean and legendary Hotel del Coronado. For the boy from Moxon's Yard who never took to New England's long, dark, snowy winters, it was like Paradise.

He led the Naval hospital radiology department to become the top-rated radiology residency program in the nation. He retired with the rank of Captain in 1990, moving with my mother to Pensacola, Florida, once again living by the sea. Finally, in 2000, at the urgings of my brother, sister, and I, they moved away from the heat and humidity of the hurricane-battered Gulf coast to Louisville, Kentucky, close to my sister and in the middle between my brother in Atlanta and me in Boston.

Tragically, in 2001, Harry was diagnosed with *Cholangiacarcinoma*—terminal cancer of the bile duct, a devastating illness. His situation was made worse by the discovery of a benign but intrusive and inoperable brain tumor that caused seizures. The medication to control his seizures sapped, but never broke his spirit. He died in Louisville, Kentucky in January 2003, just shy of what would have been his 73rd birthday.

Harry's legacy is a loving marriage of 47 years, three children, and six granddaughters of whom he was extremely proud, and a career of great accomplishment in challenging circumstances. He was a beloved and respected figure to many.

Harry accomplished so much—and yet anxiety was also a fact of his life: At times he believed that all he had could be taken away. I now know from science that poverty causes lasting damage physically at the cellular level and psychologically. Those who experience it are never entirely free of its impact.

As I reflect on his journey, what he accomplished, and the effects of the painful scars of childhood poverty on the psyche of this most wonderful man, I am committed to do what I can to enable a world of equity, opportunity, and love for all.

I reflect on his life every day—and am proud of the boy, man, and father he was: Compassionate, loving, brilliant, virtuous, mischievous, and completely inspiring. I feel blessed beyond measure to be his daughter. When I look for models of greatness in the world, my first thought is of him.

William Bailey

My grandfather retired at age 65 from Steel, Peech & Tozer. Along with my grandmother, Edna, he moved to live with us in Massachusetts when I was six. Just as he did on Moxon's Yard, because of his kindness and sincere interest in them, he became a magnet for the neighborhood children and became "Grandpa" to many of them, too. William had painful arthritis in both knees after spending decades crouching his tall frame in coal mine seams from an early age. He walked with difficulty with a cane. With no cricket to watch, he became an avid Boston Red Sox fan. He liked to watch the games on television with a sandwich and beer in hand. William developed prostate cancer and was hospitalized, dying at 77 years old. While in hospital in Boston, he tried to escape to get home to Rawmarsh and his long-deceased mother Frances. When he died my grandmother smuggled his ashes back to England and scattered them at the site of Frances' unmarked grave at Haugh Road Cemetery in Rawmarsh.

Edna Bailey

After living in Massachusetts for fifteen years, my grandmother moved to Coronado, California with my parents, living there one block from the Pacific Ocean for another 10 years. She was miles from everyone and everything she had known for most of her life. She lived to be 90 and died there in 1992. Her ashes were scattered by airplane over the Pacific—not all that far from Catalina Island, where one of the first films she saw at the Regal Cinema in 1932 was filmed.

Frances "Nanan" Bailey

Frances lived until 1956, her 80th year, having lived at the bottom of Moxon's Yard for most of her life. She remained a treasured and beloved presence in my dad's life and continued to play a much-appreciated role in the Mother's Union at St. Mary's for as long as she could. She was kind, adored my dad, and was adored by him in return. I can't help but think she must have been immensely proud of what he had accomplished. Her final years were difficult: She had a lot of pain in her legs and became house bound. Those in the family and in Rawmarsh who still remember her recall her with great fondness. We have no photos of her, so I can only imagine what she may have looked like. I've no doubt that she had a kind face that matched her disposition. She was buried in an unmarked grave at the Haugh Road Cemetery next to Rawmarsh Comprehensive School.

Horace Bailey

My dad never saw Horace again after the late 1940s—but he told us about his treasured friend many times as we grew up. Horace made a career as Medical Officer of Health for Chesterfield Borough Council, Derbyshire and lived there for many years. Much of his career focused on eradicating the slum conditions that had mired the lives of so many families including his and my dad's. He married Vivienne, a nurse also from Rawmarsh whom he met while at medical school in Sheffield. They had two daughters who entered the medical profession as doctors and a son, Tom, whose band The Thompson Twins became successful worldwide in the 1980s as MTV took the pop music world by storm with hits including *In the Name of Love, Love on Your Side,* and *Doctor, Doctor.* This is significant. My first inkling that Horace was more than a legend my dad told us about growing up was when I read a Tom Bailey interview in a magazine in the mid-1980s. It mentioned Tom's Sheffield connections and that his father was a doctor there. I told my dad what I had read, asking him if he thought there was a chance that Tom's father was Horace. My dad was interested but the conversation never went beyond that. These were pre-Internet days and making contact was far more challenging.

Eighteen years later Horace tracked down my parents' address through Sheffield University's Alumni Office and sent a letter to my dad in February 2003. It arrived a month after his death. Harry would have treasured beyond measure receiving that letter more than 50 years after they had last seen each other. For me, Horace's letter became the beginning of a beautiful new friendship. I contacted him about my desire to write this book. His response: "If you come here, I will take you wherever you want to go."

Horace was been true to his word in every sense. Over multiple visits since 2004 we scaled ladders to the bell chamber of St. Mary's in Rawmarsh and rung the bells there, went down a coal mine at the National Coal Mining Museum, gently sifted through records at the Wakefield Archives, walked the grounds of Wentworth House many times, and gone back again and again to places in Yorkshire and memory that unite our families and their lived experiences. In between we enjoyed many cups of tea and custard tarts while driving around Yorkshire and Derbyshire.

In my heart I believe that my father gave me the gift of his best friend when he could no longer be there himself. Horace was there as witness to my dad's character and childhood experiences. He played the organ and repaired these great instruments around Britain and Ireland, a lifelong interest. He was an avid reader and history buff. Upon first meeting him in 2004, I was amazed to discover that he, like my dad, was a keen orchid nurturer. There are so many ways I see why he and my dad were the best of friends.

My own friendship with Horace has been among the most important in my life. Horace lived to 93 in Sheffield, continuing to ring bells for two parish churches in Derbyshire every week until he was diagnosed with cancer and, after a mercifully brief decline, died peacefully in January 2019.

Doug "Larry" Axe

Despite the best intentions, Harry and Larry never saw each other again after Larry left school in 1946. Harry never knew what became of him—what kind of work he found or how his family fared. Their lives would take wholly different paths. But over time Harry would never forget his friend or the sadness he felt at seeing Larry's days at Mexborough

402

Grammar School end. My dad recognized his great intelligence and the exceedingly difficult challenges he faced as a teen.

Thanks to the *South Yorkshire Times* newspaper, where he saw an article about my book project, I met him in 2005. As an adult, he had shed his Three Stooges nickname. Among a range of jobs, he worked as a coal miner after leaving grammar school and, later in life, became a Labour council member in Mexborough. He married Vera, the love of his life, and raised their children there. He introduced me to one of his grandchildren, Thomas Axe, a prefect at today's Mexborough School. Thomas undoubtedly made his grandfather proud by being accepted to University of Cambridge where he earned a degree in Aerospace & Aerothermal Engineering before joining Rolls Royce Aircraft Engines in Derbyshire.

Reverend Canon George Frederick Scovell

Canon Scovell retired from Rawmarsh in 1948 at 79 years old. He had ministered to his flock through some of the nation's and West Riding's most difficult times—two world wars and the Great Slump. Scovell Avenue in Rawmarsh is named in tribute to him. Decades later he remains a much-appreciated, gratefully remembered figure in the lives of older generations who knew him in Rawmarsh and in its history. He was in a position to be an ally, an advocate, and to make a difference—and he did. I will be forever grateful for the caring and respect he showed for those among his flock who struggled the most.

Norman Chappell

Norman completed Mexbrough School two years after Harry, completed his military service, then moved to southern England to work as an engineer in the automotive industry. I met him and his Greasborough-born and -raised wife Eileen in 2005, thanks to their seeing a *Rotherham Advertiser* article about my book project. Norman survived being kidnapped by the Irish Republican Army in the 1970s when he worked for an auto manufacturer in Northern Ireland. Like Horace, he became one of my "Yorkshire Dads" as a result of writing this book. He had a wonderful warmth, wit, and delightful storytelling style.

Derek Cooper

Derek and family moved away from Moxon's Yard after the end of World War II. He returned to Rawmarsh and married Joan from Pottery Street, a block over from Moxon's Yard. Despite my grandfather William's urgings that he not "go down the mine, young Dek," he became a coal miner and lived his life in Rawmarsh. I became close to Derek and Joan thanks to meeting them in 2005 as a result of the *Rotherham Advertiser* article.

John Edward Dyson

My great-grandfather died in 1956 and shares a tombstone with his beloved wife, my great grandmother Lucy. He never married Emily, who was already married when she moved in with him as housekeeper after Lucy's death. They had three children together. Edna loved her half siblings, but what was then a highly scandalous arrangement between her father and Emily led to school-yard taunts that scarred her and her siblings. I am gladly connected to all the Dyson offspring. We are all family, including Emily.

Ted Hughes

Upon leaving Mexborough, Ted Hughes completed his military service in the Royal Air Force, then moved onto Cambridge University, where he pursued his love of poetry. At Cambridge he met, then married American poet Sylvia Plath, author of *The Bell Jar*, with whom he had a well-documented tumultuous and doomed relationship. Ted briefly lived close by to my dad in Massachusetts in the late 1950s, but their paths did not cross. He was named Britain's poet laureate in 1984 and received the Order of Merit from H.M. Queen Elizabeth II, accepting it at Buckingham Palace two weeks before dying of cancer at age 68 in 1998. My dad was immensely proud of his schoolmate's accomplishments and considered him to be a far more positive figure than portrayed after Plath's tragic death.

Dedication and Gratitude

Harry Bailey was the first great hero of my life. His compassion, empathy, and courage lit up the world. He is forever present in my life—and was a father and man of rich talents—truly a Renaissance man. I dedicate this book to him with love and gratitude. I also dedicate it to the world's children, each of whom deserves the opportunity to live in peace and reach their fullest intellectual and spiritual potential in conditions that foster their well-being.

This book is also dedicated with deepest thanks and love to: Dr. Horace Bailey, whom I now count as one of my own dearest friends. Soon after my dad's death he tracked down my dad's address in the United States and wrote to him. My dad never saw the letter, but I somehow think he had something to do with my meeting Horace 55 years after the two friends last saw each other. When I told Horace I wanted to write a book about my dad's childhood, he replied, "If you come to England, I will take you wherever you want to go."

He did just that, with us both scaling ladders into bell tower at St. Mary's, accompanying me to the old and new Mexborough schools, going down a coal mine at the National Coal Mining Museum, taking me to the West Riding's archives at the Wakefield Archives to study old count records while wearing cloth gloves to protect them, visiting Smedley's Hydro in Derbyshire (now Derbyshire County Council offices), where my great grandmother Lucy (Thompson) Dyson fought for every breath trying to overcome tuberculosis, to parish churches throughout Yorkshire and Derbyshire, and yes, for plentiful tea breaks and retail therapy stops, too. Horace has an incredibly vibrant mind with a rich knowledge of music, archaeology, local history, medicine, and astronomy.

I dedicate this book to my grandparents, William and Edna (Dyson) Bailey and to my great grandmothers, my dad's beloved Nanan Frances (Wilson) Bailey and to Lucy Thompson Dyson, whose spirit is alive with us still. I learned so much about each of them in speaking with those who knew them.

I also dedicate this book to the memory of Edgar Makin, whose friendship and tragic death affected my dad deeply.

Edgar was, in his short life, a wonderful presence who made my dad feel special.

I am thankful to Tommy Jacques for his generosity of spirit—and for his quick thinking when danger presented itself. I'm deeply thankful to David Jacques, his son, who read my story in the Rotherham *Advertiser* from his home in Spain and sent me photos and detailed notes on my dad and Moxon's Yard history—an unexpected and wonderful gift.

My Bailey and Dyson cousins: Val (Payne) Murray and Les Payne for their empathy, understanding, hospitality, and love in supporting my quest. From visits to Wentworth House and the George & Dragon Inn to visits to Walker Scales' butcher shop in Rawmarsh and the former Mexborough Grammar School and current Mexborough Comprehensive School, they encouraged me and sustained me when my emotions felt most raw.

My cousin Lauren Payne Walklet for encouraging me and learning alongside me in my quest.

Jack Payne and Ernest Payne, my dad's older cousins who made a sometimes-lonely only child feel valued every time they played with him. I first met Ernest Payne in 1970 when we briefly visited his house in Rawmarsh when I was nine. He had a pile of coal in his small back yard. I asked him if I could have a piece of it. He must have thought that was a strange request. It turned out to be foreshadowing for me. Little did I know then that I would write this book. Forty-eight years later I still have that lump of coal in my bedside table drawer.

The Reverend George Frederick Scovell, who not only commanded respect because of his position in society, but also became a vital ally to my dad and beloved presence in the lives of so many Rawmarsh families. He recognized the talents in my dad and Horace Bailey. His caring for the most vulnerable in Rawmarsh made a profound difference in countless lives. I am one of the beneficiaries closing in on 90 years later.

John Fisher at Mexborough School—a most inspiring and refreshing teacher for a generation of students. He saw my dad's promise and encouraged his love of writing, a love my dad in turn inspired in me—and to all teachers who understand that their job is not to break children, but to cultivate them and help them see and realize their talents.

To Mr. Willey, the butcher who entrusted my dad with the important work of caring for and properly feeding the pigs that

410

fed so many households in Rawmarsh at a time when food was in short supply.

David Dyson and his lovely wife Christine, whose strong interest in family history and own accomplishments as the second family member to go to university inspire me. I also dedicated this book to Anthea Goodman and to the memory of her husband, Philip, who was still with us when I started to research this book.

Thanks to Harry's and Horace's St. Mary's Youth Group friend and school mate Betty Wright. Thank you to St. Mary's, Choral Director John Allot, organist William Blythe, and church warden and family friend Frank Pickering. More recently at St. Mary's, to Joan Brookes, who, as church warden, embraced my quest, when I first returned to Rawmarsh in 2004.

One of the greatest gifts I've experienced in writing this book and in my life is the chance I've had to meet my dad's childhood friends. When he did, I feel like he gave me four surrogate Yorkshire dads to stand in for him after his death:

Norman Chappell and his wife Eileen--whose warmth and generosity of time taking me to various parts of Yorkshire enriched my understanding. Norman was the one who spilled the beans on the carbon urinate gas.

Doug "Larry" Axe, whose influence helped me craft some of the beginning of the book—and his grandson, Thomas Axe, a top student and prefect at the new Mexborough Comprehensive School, who graciously gave me a tour of the school.

Derek and Joan Cooper—who welcomed me into their home and hearts.

John Turner, Ron Liversidge, his wife Gwynn, and their daughter and son-in-law Jane and Ray Hearne, Joan Brookes—all who shared stories about my dad and their lives in Rawmarsh.

My dear cousins Elsie Astbury, Irene Bailey, Catherine Bailey, Dorothy Manners, and Marina England for telling me like it was—being willing to re-visit the sometime painful past and illuminate the joyful.

Lee Siggs of the *South Yorkshire Times;* Michelle Adamson, photographer for the *SY Times* and Sheffield's *The Star* newspaper; and Michele Vincent and Doug Melloy of

The Rotherham Advertiser for running stories that connected me to my dad's childhood friends and so many more generous Rawmarsh and Rotherham people who took an interest in my book and sent me helpful insights and encouragement. All of them have enriched my life more than they know. Ruth Toothill of the Carnegie Library, Rawmarsh, where my dad spent many happy hours. Local historian Tony Dodsworth, whose captivating local history book *Around Rawmarsh and Parkgate* and lecture at the Rotherham Public Library, brought Rawmarsh's past to life for me.

Kenneth Francis, my underground guide at the National Coal Mining Museum and the museum for the important work they do of preserving and interpreting our history.

Carol Kay, librarian of Mexborough Comprehensive School, who found my father's student records and presented me with copies of them and Hilary Shenton, Secretary of the Medical School, for doing the same. The Wakefield Archives, for organizing and caring for the West Riding's historic records.

Ruth Stanley and Helen Scarlett of Sheffield University.

Walker Scales, who was in his 90s when I met him in 2004 and still ran his butcher's shop and made his own pork pies. He did *not* remember my dad, but, astonishingly, remembered my *grandfather* William as a "right stiff lad"—or tall— teenage boy in the early years of the 20th century.

The Boy Scouts troop and youth group at St. Mary's. Both enriched my dad's life.

And now, to the those closest to me who made this all possible: My husband Tom Boulet, for his love, support, helpful feedback and perspectives, and patience over may years as I've researched and written this story and hit the occasional technology glitch. My daughters Liza Boulet and Gwen Boulet for their love and for accompanying me on trips back to Yorkshire to fulfill my quest. They all light up my life and inspired me throughout this journey. To dear friend Elizabeth Price, who, as my friend from the age of 8, knew and loved my dad, understands the importance of cups of tea, and reading my draft and shared her ample wisdom to make it better.

To Jeff Nally for wonderful friendship, coaching me, and believing in me as I set out on this journey. He read my draft thoughtfully and his insight helped to make the story better.

To Cathy Fyock, my wise, inspiring, and patient book coach, for knowing when and how to encourage me. To Fred Johnson, Colonel Robert Campbell and Barbara Sadek for reviewing my draft and offering thoughtful feedback.

Ted Price, Gillian and Simon Sherrington, Kathy and Roger Tunsley, Laura Parker Roerden, Deborah Dumaine, Nancy Breuer, Navi Vernon, Elvin Serrano, Barbara Lanebrown, Gretchen Hunt, Dior Cotten, Ken Howard, Annie McQuilken, Gregory North, and Stephanie Thompson for encouraging me.

To my mother Kathleen Bailey for shedding light on my dad's life and to my sister Megan (Bailey) Gerdes for her family history research.

Growing up in Massachusetts, I had several great teachers in my life, who affirmed and encouraged my love of writing and history. They, like John Fisher in my dad's life, touched my life profoundly: My fourth-grade teacher Cora Joy Thompson of the Westwood Public Schools, who met me at

415

the school bus one morning when I was nine years old to tell me how much she liked a creative essay I wrote. That gesture made me believe in myself and cemented my love of writing. Other great teachers encouraged me, too: Evelyn Lindquist, John Sloan, and Evelyn Malm of Westwood Public Schools. Also, Margaret Metzger and Bradford Wright of Brookline Public Schools, and, at university, John Rosser of Boston College.

Diane Bailey-Boulet

June 2020

Bibliography and Reference Sources

Axe, Doug. *History of the Axe Family in Mexborough.*

Bailey, Catherine. Black Diamonds: The Rise and Fall of an English Dynasty. *Penguin Books, 2008.*

Battye. David. *Sheffield Dialect and Folklore Since the Second World War: A Dying Tradition.* ALD Design & Print, Sheffield, 2009.

Baylies, Carolyn. *The History of the Yorkshire Miners: 1881-1918.* Routledge, 1993.

Berridge, Virginia. "The NHS: what can we learn from history?" *History Extra.* historyextra.com. BBC History Magazine, 2009.

"Blitz." Wikipedia. www.wikipedia.com.

Brass Brand Results, BrassBandResults.co.uk

British Council. "We of the West Riding." *British Council Film Archive,* 1945. *YouTube,* https://www.youtube.com/watch?v=WohhLX_YLlE

Brown, Frances. *Fairfield Folk: A History of the British Fairground and Its People.* The Malvern Publishing Company Limited, 1988.

Cinema Treasures. *Cinema Treasures.* cinematreasures.org

Dearmer, Percey, et al. *The Oxford Book of Carols.* Oxford University Press, 1964.

Dodsworth, Anthony. Around Rawmarsh and Parkgate. Images of England 2002.

Ellis, Norma. *South Yorkshire at Work on Old Picture Postcards.* Reflections of a Bygone Age, 2006.

Ely, Steve. "Hughes There: A Poet's Journey Through Mexborough, Yorkshire Post." *Ted Hughes's South Yorkshire: Made in Mexborough.* Yorkshire Post, 2015.

Feinstein, Elain. *Ted Hughes: The Life of a Poet.* W.W. Norton & Company, 2003.

Freese, Barbara. *Coal: A Human History.* Penguin Books, 2003.

"German Prisoners of War in Britain." Radio Marconi. radiomarconi.com.

"Haugh Road Rawmarsh Senior School, South Yorkshire." *WW2 People's War: An Archive of World War Two Memories.* BBC, 2014.

"History of Coal Miners/Great Britain/2.3 1920-4." *Wikipedia.* www.wikipedia.com

Imperial War Museums. "8 Facts About Clothes Rationing in Britain During the Second World War." *IWM,* www.iwm.org.uk

Jones, Mevyn. *South Yorkshire Yesterday: Glimpses of the Past.* Smith Settle, 2003.

Just Imagine. Directed by David Butler, performances by El Brendel, John Garrick, and Maureen O'Sullivan, Fox Film Corporation, 1930.

Keefe, Zachary. "What is Soot and Why is it Dangerous?" *Cashins & Associates Blog.* blog.cashins.com.

"Mastoiditis." Wikipedia. www.wikipedia.com.

McIvor, Arthur and Ronald Johnston. *Miner's Lung: A History of Dust Disease in British Coal Mines.* Routledge, 2016.

Munford, Anthony P. *Iron & Steel Town: An Industrial History of Rotherham.* Sutton Publishing Limited, 2003.

Orwell, George. *The Road to Wigan Pier.* Left Book Club, 1937 and Harcourt Brace, 1958.

Palmer, John. "Smedley's Hydro Handbook." *Wirksworth Parish Records 1600 – 1900,* wirksworth.org.uk.

"Sheffield Blitz." Wikipedia. www.wikipedia.com.

Supple B. "The British Coal Industry between the Wars." In: Digby A., Feinstein C., Jenkins D. (eds) *New Directions in Economic and Social History.* Palgrave, London, 1992. https://doi.org/10.1007/978-1-349-22448-7_14

Turvey, Roger. *The Depression Years in Wales and England, 1930-1939.* WJEC, 2013.

"Vintage Fairground Games." *Traditional Fair.* www.traditionalfair.co.uk.

Waller, Maureen. *London 1945: Life in the Debris of War.* St. Martin's Griffin, 2004

Wentworth Woodhouse. "Fascinating Facts." *Wentworth Woodhouse.* Wentworthwoodhouse.org.uk

West Yorkshire Federation of Women's Institutes. *West Yorkshire Within Living Memory.* Countryside Books, 1996.

"William Wentworth-Fitzwilliam, 7th Earl Fitzwilliam." *Wikipedia.* www.wikipedia.com

Wilson, Frances. "Love and Scandal Amidst the Coal Dust." *The Telegraph*, 11 March 2007.

Music Playlist for
Poverty to Possibility

Alexander, Cecil Frances. "Once In Royal David's City."
1848. Performed by Kings College Choir, *Nine Lesson &
Carols*, 2012.

Champion, Thomas. "Ever Weather-Beaten Sail." 1603.

Dunkerly, William and Alexander Reinagle. "In Christ There
is No East or West."

Edward Elgar, *Salut d'Amour Op. 12* (Liebesgrub), My dad's
"set piece" on the piano as a teenager.

Finzi, Gerald. "Romance for String Orchestra in E Flat
Major." *Opus 11*. From *Finzi Clarinet Concertos*,
Northern Symphonia Orchestra, Howard Griffith.

Gerald Finzi, Five Bagatelles, Op. 23A, I, Prelude.
Performed by Northern Symphonia Orchestra.

Handel, George Frederik. "Hallelujah Chorus." *The Messiah.*

Lyte, Henry F. "Abide With Me."

Mak, BB. "Out of My Heart." *Into Your Head.*

Thompson Twins, et al. "You Take Me Up." *Into the Gap.*

About the Author

Diane Bailey-Boulet is a British-American writer raised in Boston, Massachusetts. Her family hails from Yorkshire and Lancashire, England. From childhood visits to England to see family and while living there in her early 20s she became keenly interested in British history and understanding her own family's stories. An Anglican choral music lover since she was a child, Diane read history at Boston College, earning a Bachelor of Arts degree. She also lived in and studied at Bath University (UK) and studied Teaching English to Speakers of Other Languages (TESOL) at the master's level at Boston University's School of Education.

Diane is keenly interested in telling stories that link past and present, especially as a means of advocating for the value and importance of inclusion and opportunity for all. Her stories from the past illuminate the still contemporary need to challenge and solve the injustices of poverty, environmental degradation, and their brutal impacts on children, their families, and communities worldwide.

When she's not writing or speaking on these topics, Diane loves to travel, cook, make tea, read, putter in her garden, and volunteer on the boards of organizations committed to enabling opportunity and wellbeing. Andrea Levy, Isabelle Allende, Jane Austen, Charles Dickens, and Howard Spring are among her favorite authors.

Diane is married and draws inspiration from her husband and two daughters. She currently lives in the United States and considers herself to be a citizen of the world.